REALLY DANGEROUS IDEAS!

By the same author

Aboriginal Self-Determination: the Whiteman's Dream
Right Social Justice: Better Ways to Help the Poor.

really dangerous ideas

Edited by Gary Johns

with a Foreword by Judith Sloan

connorcourt
PUBLISHING

Published in 2013 by Connor Court Publishing Pty Ltd

Connor Court Publishing Pty Ltd.
PO Box 1
Ballan VIC 3342
sales@connorcourt.com
www.connorcourt.com

ISBN: 9781922168092 (pbk.)

Cover design by Ian James

Printed in Australia

CONTENTS

Foreword

Judith Sloan

As a dangerous idea is to inner-city, progressive trendies, offensive and unworkable tosh is to everybody else. That is why I like the idea of very dangerous ideas which accept the importance of institutions, are wary of big government solutions and are respectful of individual freedoms.

Dangerous ideas are utterly predictable. Inequality is increasing; the environment is deteriorating; taxes need to be raised; racism is endemic; religion – at least Christianity – is dangerous; all men are misogynists. These are the sorts of propositions on which the holders of dangerous ideas agree, mostly with no investigation or empirical proof required.

By contrast, very dangerous ideas are many and varied. I can find myself agreeing with some and not others. I do not think Australia should become a superpower but I am happy to read why this could be a good idea. Is it really true that all intellectual contributions are pointless? Again, I am not sure, but again I am very happy to learn why intellectuals may not matter. Coal to oil? Again, not sure.

But when it comes to downsizing Canberra, abolishing the Human Rights Commission and privatising the ABC, I am nearly all the way there.

The real beauty of this volume is that it is no dialogue of the deaf. There is a range of opinions, clearly expressed but not crammed into a neat, one-size-fits-all box.

But there is a recurring theme in quite a few of the papers. People legitimately hold a variety of views; people make bad decisions from time to time; governments are not really there to help us. If these are very dangerous ideas, I am signing on.

February 2013

Professor Judith Sloan

Contributing Economics Editor

The Australian

Really Dangerous Ideas: Introduction

Gary Johns

The inspiration for this book of Really Dangerous Ideas comes from the Festival of Dangerous Ideas (FODI). The Sydney Opera House and the St James Ethics Centre have hosted FODI for four years. It appears that the festival organisers deem an idea dangerous when it proposes to undermine or sweep away an institution or convention regardless of merit. Naming the ideas dangerous is an exercise in irony. Most of the ideas proposed at the festival are indeed dangerous, for the mayhem they would create if ever implemented. It is time to fight back. We propose that *really* dangerous ideas are those that defend the best institutions and customs. It may well be that what really matters are not the latest fashions among the intellectual salons of the nation (and their propensity to destroy and undermine), but those conversations and deeds among the toilers and creators that occur outside.

Although the FODI organisers try to canvass ideas that appeal across the political spectrum, they are about as balanced as ABC1 television's *Q&A* and as subtle as, 'when did you stop beating your wife?' For example, *Israel is an Apartheid State* was a nice little starter in the 2012 Festival. Ilan Pappe, an Israeli, was invited to speak. He is the author of *The Ethnic Cleansing of Palestine*. It may be clear from the title of his book that he is somewhat one-sided on the subject. We have invited former Labor federal minister Barry Cohen to present a more balanced case in this collection, in his chapter *22 Arab Countries, One Goal: Destruction of Israel*.

Abolish Private Schools was another FODI topic, and duly the FODI invited Pasi Sahlberg, Director General of Centre for International Mobility and Cooperation in Helsinki, Finland, to expound the virtues of a system without any private schools. Ah, the Soviets are back! We have invited the inimitable Kevin Donnelly to expound on why *School Choice Matters to Poor Students*, just in case anyone should forget that the non-government sector is the fastest growing and most successful school provider in Australia.

According to FODI, *All Australians are Racists*. Randa Abdel-Fattah of Sydney, described as a lawyer, writer and 'human rights activist of Palestinian and Egyptian heritage' along with an archetypal angry Aborigine were asked by FODI to expound on this terrible indictment of Australian society. No doubt they agreed to boost the powers of Australia's race laws and the number of bureaucrats in the Australian Human Rights Commission, which Gary Johns counters by arguing to *Abolish the Human Rights Commission*. We decided to invite Kerryn Pholi, a former Aboriginal activist, who has given up the game of playing victim and angry Aborigine, and instead she asks *Does Respect Matter?*

Anzac Day: Best We Forget, is another FODI special and has loads of undergraduate charm. Marilyn Lake, apparently 'an Australian historian best known for her work on the effects of the military and war on Australian civil society', was wheeled in to do the job. She bewails the militarisation of Australia's history with nary a thought to what might have happened if Australia had lost a war or two. A good dose of understanding *Why We Need Nation States* and their role in securing democracy by our David Martin Jones should serve as a reminder that all of the rights enjoyed by citizens in democracies were won by defeating, by military means, fascists and communists.

But, like the ABC and the FODI, there is always a guest enemy, in this case Chris Leithner who argues that the panic and bust of the Global Financial Crisis came about because government regulation stifles the free market. Our Frank Milne is not so extreme, but warns regulators to be alert and alarmed, in his essay *Financial Complacency in the Face of Three Economic Crises*.

No FODI would be complete without a greenie and in *The End of Growth* by Richard Heinberg, a journalist in the 'fields of natural resource consumption and sustainability', we observe the usual doom and gloom. Fortunately, in this collection, we have Eric Jones who argues that *Biodiversity Does Not Matter: Revealed Biodiversity Matters*, or, how humans value the environment as opposed to having loads of it, is what really matters. And Heinberg could do with a second dose of reality, supplied by David Archibald in *Australia Needs Liquid Fuel Security*. Archibald is bold enough to suggest that converting coal to oil is within reach and in Australia's interest.

Who Owns Australia is a confronting topic, but alas, it had nothing to do with foreign investment, instead the time was devoted to Michael Anderson (Nyoongar Ghurradjong Murri Ghillar) who apparently in the 1970s was appointed by his peers as 'the first Aboriginal ambassador to white Australia'. We did not have the heart to indulge that nonsense, but we did invite Asher Judah to set the record straight that *Foreign Investment Matters to Australian Workers* (for Aboriginal workers too). Of course, we could not compete with Germaine Greer, whose FODI session was *How Many Dangerous Ideas can One Person Have?* We suggest that, in her case, at least one too many. We recommend she read the homely Richard Lyons on *Family is the Fundamental Unit of Society*.

Perhaps our favourite FODI participant is philosopher Matthew Liao, Director of the Bioethics Program and an Associate Professor in the Centre for Bioethics in the Department of Philosophy at New York University, whose session was entitled, *Engineer Humans to Stop Climate Change*. God knows what he is on, but a good dose of our James Franklin in *Science Matters in a Post-modern World* and Ian Harper in *Religion Matters for Faith, Hope and Love* may set him and his followers straight.

In previous years FODI has hosted such luminaries as our own Cassandra Wilkinson and John Humphreys, but they rather suspected that they were guest enemies, or were there to make the place appear 'balanced'. Fortunately for our readers, they have written in this volume, respectively, on *Australia Should Become a Superpower* and *Downsize Canberra: Remove Federal Income Tax*, which really are level-headed. These sensible ideas contrast with what one may describe as the usual suspects, such as FODI stars including: Julian Assange about how *Wikileaks Has Not Gone Far Enough* and American novelist and vegetarian, Jonathan Safran Foer, who claims that our lust for cheap animal protein has made the torture and degradation of living creatures an unseen but integral part of life and that we should no longer ignore the costs. We did not have the stomach for such insensitiveness and provided no counter, but I suspect there are few 'ideologically motivated' vegetarians on our slate of writers.

FODI star, Slovenian philosopher and apparently one of the world's leading public intellectuals, Slavoj Zizek, suggests society should *Let Us Be Realists and Demand the Impossible: Communism*. Trouble is, Slavoj really believes it! Perhaps he should read our Greg Melleuish on *Intellectuals Do Not Matter*. Once he has read that, a good antidote to this 'Milk Bar Marxist' is Peter Day's *Why the World Needs the Anglosphere* and Michael James' *European Union as Self-aggrandisement*. Slavoj may then return to ABC1 *Q&A* and make sense, for once. And as for the ABC, Tom Switzer argues that the time has come to *Privatise the ABC*.

Who are the people who attend FODI and believe the nonsense they are fed? Clearly, those who forsake the world of markets and profit, who forsake religion, except for environmentalism, who forsake science, except in the service of climate change abatement policies. They are the people we call, and they also call, Progressives. Our Tim Wilson has something to say about this in *Progressives: Philosophy Adrift Without an Anchor*.

The proposition in this book is that not much progress occurs when Progressives rule the policy roost. Unfortunately, according to our Miranda Kiraly's *Bittersweet Charity*, too many have invaded the charity sector. Charities once eschewed big government, but now spend much of their time and donors' funds lobbying for more of it.

These are beaut little essays, written in an opinion style, easy to digest, indeed really dangerous. Enjoy.

PS We intend to publish a collection every year!

1

Australia Needs Liquid Fuel Security

David Archibald

The Australian Government recently released an Energy White Paper. The most important thing it had to say was that the Australian Government was reneging on its commitment to hold 90 days of stocks of oil, as it is required to do under the International Energy Agency agreement. Honouring that treaty would cost more than $300 million per annum at the current oil price. A far more insightful document was a short article in *The Financial Times* published shortly after the White Paper. 'In 2000, when there were eight refineries in Australia, only 5 per cent of fuel was imported – equivalent to less than 100,000 b/d (barrels per day). Fuel imports rose to nearly a quarter of total demand by 2010, or 320,000 b/d, as consumption increased and one refinery closed.' Royal Dutch Shell and Caltex have announced the closure of two ageing refineries near Sydney, at one stroke reducing by almost a third the country's refining capacity. This will push Australia's imports of petrol, diesel, jet fuel and fuel oil to 640,000 b/d by 2015 – about two-thirds of total demand.

Australian energy security is at risk

Martin Ferguson, Minister for Resources and Energy, has said that the refinery closures 'will not jeopardise Australia's energy security'. That is plain wrong. Australian energy security is at extreme risk. For the Minister to say so, however, would mean that the Government would have to do something about it. As it turns out, to solve the problem of Australia's extreme risk in energy security, the Government does not have to physically do anything or spend funds. All it has to do is to repeal the carbon tax and allow others to do what is required.

Were Australian Governments always so indifferent to liquid fuel security? Not at all. When the Bass Strait oilfields were found in the 1960s, they could not be economically developed in competition with the low price of Middle Eastern crude at the time. The solution was to impose a surcharge on the price of petrol for a number of years until the international oil price rose to above that required for commerciality. Before the discovery of oil in Bass Strait, the Federal Government used to subsidise oil exploration. That was two generations ago. What kind of painful experiences did that generation of Australians go through that they were quite happy to subsidise oil producers and oil explorers at a time when oil was cheap and plentiful? Does Australia want to repeat those painful experiences?

Australia's political leaders have not always been living in a fool's paradise on the subject of liquid fuel security. In 2005, Kim Beazley, while then leader of the Federal Labor Opposition asked, in an address to the Australian Institute of Company Directors, 'As Australians queue for petrol at around $4.00, $5.00 potentially up to $10.00 a litre further down the track, the questions will be: how had our governments not seen the writing on the wall?'

Just as the oil price in Australia was once so low that oil production required a subsidy, the oil price is now high enough that a solution to Australia's liquid fuel security problem is in plain sight and within grasp. The solution is the development of a coal-to-liquids industry. Coal-to-liquids (CTL) requires an oil price of $70 per barrel to be economic. The oil price paid in this part of the world is Tapis which, at December 2012, is $113 per barrel – well in excess of that required for CTL to be viable. The CTL process does not need high quality export coal. Rocks will burn in pure oxygen down to 10 per cent carbon. There is a lot of low-grade coal in Australia that is stranded due to its high ash content or high water content. The CTL process yields 2.2 barrels per tonne of coal for high-grade coal down to 0.6 barrels per tonne of brown coal. The mother lode of brown coal in Australia is the Latrobe Valley. Each billion tonnes of brown coal will yield 600 million barrels of liquid fuels. At that rate, Australia needs to consume about seven billion tonnes of coal to equal the oil that the Bass Strait oilfields have yielded. On the basis that the Latrobe Valley resource is 112 billion tonnes, that would make 67 billion barrels of liquid fuels to keep Australia's farms and factories running. That is the natural fate of that resource.

South Africa was a pioneer of CTL in the post-WWII era. The company that did that, Sasol, has now forsaken CTL to pursue a Gas-to-Liquids (GTL) plant in the US on the expectation that US gas prices will remain low from shale gas drilling. That is a big mistake. The international LNG market started tightening when the oil price started rising in 2004 and, by 2008, the LNG market in Asia was trading at the oil price in energy equivalent terms. On top of that, natural gas can be used directly in vehicles as compressed natural gas (CNG). So the GTL process takes an energy source that can be used directly as an automotive fuel and is priced at the oil price on the international market to make a denser fuel at much the same price but loses 33 per cent of the energy content in doing that. Natural gas has a far better home as LNG feedstock (only 6 per cent energy loss) than as GTL feedstock. GTL is a red herring for Australia.

Synthetic fuel

There is a synthetic fuels plant that is pertinent to Australian needs. This is the Great Plains Synfuels plant in North Dakota. It was conceived under the Carter Administration as a response to the second oil shock of 1980. As with most Carter initiatives, the intention was good but the execution was flawed due to a poor understanding of the real world. At the time, it was thought that the US had a shortage of natural gas, so the Great Plains plant was set up to make synthetic natural gas instead of diesel and jet fuel. That perceived shortage was simply due to bad Federal legislation on the price of interstate trade in natural gas. Nobody explored for gas because it was unprofitable to produce. The shortage was artificial. As soon as the Natural Gas Act of 1938 was repealed, gas production returned. For the last 28 years, that plant has been burning 18,000 tonnes per day of brown coal, which could make 20,000 barrels per day of liquid fuels. How many such plants does Australia need to replace its current level of imports? The answer is 25 for starters. More than that and Australia can export as well. Australia will have a higher standard of living and be safer.

What are the Chinese doing about CTL? They are going gangbusters. As at mid-2011, there were eight active CTL projects in China – three operational and five under construction or planning. The total production capacity of these efforts to date is 600,000 barrels per day, which is much the same as Australia needs to install in the near term. The Chinese can be very practical people. Only 70 per cent of Chinese wind farms are connected to the power grid. The wind farms were paid for by the Europeans under carbon offset programs, but nearly a third of them were not worthwhile connecting to the grid, so the Chinese did not bother.

At the current Tapis oil price of $118 per barrel (February 2013), Australian refined product imports at 640,000 barrels per day would cost about $84 million dollars per day. That is $30 billion dollars per annum that would be taken out of the Australian economy, shrinking it and making all Australians poorer. Instead of that bleak future, CTL plants could be built in every Australian state to create a very diverse and secure supply base. Diesel, petrol and jet fuel could be made in plants close to the markets they will serve, reducing transport costs.

There are no laws specifically stopping the building of CTL plants in Australia. Screening economic analysis suggests that CTL plants would enjoy a very high rate of return on capital. So why are they not being built? The impediment is Australia's carbon tax. No new coal-fired power stations have been built on the east coast of Australia for years as a consequence of the anticipation of that tax. There has been discussion about forcing the closure of existing brown coal-fired power stations in the Latrobe Valley. The same government that brought in the carbon tax is quite happily allowing and encouraging the export of Australian coal. Currently that is at the rate of 400 million tonnes per annum, which through CTL plants would make 2.4 million barrels per day of diesel and jet fuel. Just converting what Australia currently exports in the raw state would give Australia energy security for generations to come.

Carbon tax misplaced

If the carbon tax is holding back Australia from a wealthier and far more secure future, and the carbon tax itself was instituted to combat global warming, how is global warming going? First, let's examine observational evidence. The world is no warmer than it was 15 years ago despite eight per cent more carbon dioxide in the atmosphere. According to global warming theory, that extra eight per cent should have caused some warming. It has not. The observational period is long enough to say that this result has invalidated the theory of global warming. Depending upon how the science is done, carbon dioxide contributes to the warming of the planet, but at the current level of 392 parts per million (ppm), the effect is minuscule and is lost in the noise of the climate system. That does accord with what has happened to the world's climate for the last 15 years. The world did warm in the second half of the 20th century up to 15 years ago. That begs the question: what did warm the world if it was not carbon dioxide? The answer is rather obvious – the sun. The sun does vary in its activity and in the second half of the 20th century, it was more active than at any time in the previous 8,000 years.

All in all, it seems that a discredited climate theory is holding Australia back from a wealthier and far more secure future. All Australia has to do to achieve that wealthier and far more secure future is to discard that discredited theory of global warming. Necessity will ensure that that will be done in any case. The global warming theory had a similar effect on the values and utility of land at near sea level in NSW. The residents on and around Lake Macquarie were particularly affected. In response, they elected a mayor in Newcastle who campaigned against global warming theory and its affect on property vales. The NSW State Government took note of that and instructed the NSW Chief Scientist to issue a report stating that sea level rise was not an issue of concern. That is the first instance of global warming theory in retreat in Australia. The same principle – that global warming theory is doing too much damage to be allowed to stand – should be applied on a national scale. Australia's CTL industry, which will be the saviour of the nation, will then flourish.

2

22 Arab Countries, One Goal: Destruction of Israel

Barry Cohen

Great hopes were held for the *Arab Spring* to bring about freedom and democracy in the Arab world, for at the time only one Arab country had the vaguest idea of what democracy was all about. And Lebanon had hardly been a stunning success. Tunisia got the *Arab Spring* off to a reasonable start with only 338 killed, but what followed was horrendous. Those who have doubts about the success of the fight for freedom that followed should cast their eyes over the numbers killed in the first two years of the *Arab Spring*. In view of the lack of experience in running a 'free' society the following makes for interesting reading.

Arab-on-Arab violence

The Federal Parliamentary Library provided the estimates of those killed. Tunisia 338; Bahrain 114; Egypt 846; Libya 25,000–30,000; Yemen 2,000; Syria 60,000 plus; and nine other countries 116. That adds up to at least 88,414 Arabs who were killed by other Arabs by January 2013. If you think that is a lot, ponder the numbers who have perished in the Middle East since Israel was established in 1948. The so-called 'minor' conflagrations in Algeria, Sudan, Darfur, Iraq, Iran, Lebanon, Afghanistan, Somalia, Jordan, Chad, Syria, Turkey and Yemen resulted in 8.5 million deaths. By contrast, the number killed in the Israel/Arab conflicts since 1948 were 85,000. The ratio of Arab-on-Arab violence to Arab-on-Israeli violence is 100 to 1.

Imagine the toll if the Arabs did not like each other, or what they would do to the Israelis if they ever got the chance. While tens of thousands of Arabs were dying at the hands of their fellow Arabs did anyone notice the Progressive Left marching through the streets protesting the slaughter? They might have if they had not been so involved in the loss of 161 Palestinians who died when Israel decided to stop the firing of thousands of rockets by Hamas into Israel from Gaza.

This is where the hypocrisy of the Left is so breathtaking. The latest estimates of the number of Syrians who have died at the hands of fellow Syrians is believed to be in excess of 60,000 and rising. What did we hear from the Left when this massacre was occurring? The sounds of silence. Where were the 'boycotts, sanctions and divestment' of all those Arab nations who had killed tens of thousands of fellow Arabs? If they said anything, it was to condemn Israel for daring to defend itself against Arab rocket attacks. They did not even have the chutzpah to use their favourite word for Israel's 'disproportionate' defence.

It is obvious to those who have taken the time to study the history of the Middle East conflict and the years of trying to reach an agreement for a genuine peace that it is 'a bridge too far'. There are Arabs who genuinely desire peace but there are millions, particularly amongst the Muslim Brotherhood, who glorify death and they would never surrender their right to martyrdom by failing to attempt to destroy Israel. Israel's only way of satisfying them is to commit national suicide – and that is not likely. One Holocaust in a lifetime is enough. The national motto of 'Never Again' says it all. Those who have heard Israel's genuine peace offers and seen them refused should study the disparity between the number of Arabs and Jews in the Middle East.

Worldwide the number of Muslims is approximately 1.2 billion while the number of Jews is around 14 million. The numbers of Arabs in the Middle East is approximately 250 million. Despite the huge disparity, Israel, with one of the best defence systems in the world, has been able to repel 65 years of attempts by Muslims to destroy it. It has been said many times that the Arabs can lose a hundred wars but Israel cannot afford to lose one. If they do, they know what would happen. Throughout the centuries Jews have learnt one very important lesson: if anyone says that it is their intention to slaughter them, they had better believe them. Before WWII, the Jewish population worldwide was approximately 18 million. After the massacre of six million in the Holocaust and the war of independence against the Arabs, there were just 12 million left. It has taken 65 years for the numbers to return to 14 million. One should not be surprised at the hypocrisy of the Left as they still have not had the courage to apologise for their support of Stalin and Mao who between them massacred almost 100 million of their own people as a means of cleaning out the 'undesirables' who were undermining the 'Revolution'.

Having lost the battle and refusing to apologise, the Left's latest blind spot has been the Middle East. There are 22 Arab countries with one goal – the destruction of Israel. It is a solution to the conflict but not one with a particular appeal to Israelis. The conflict between Arabs and Jews has continued unabated since the 1870s and with greater intensity since the United Nations established the two states in 1947 – one Arab and one Jewish. Israel accepted the United Nations (UN) decision, even though it was well short of their demands. The Arabs rejected the UN proposal. Egypt, Jordan, Syria, Iraq and Lebanon attacked Israel with help from Saudi Arabia, Yemen, Libya and Palestinian terrorists.

There have been numerous attempts to bring about peace with cease fires, truces, amnesties and peace accords. Every one of these conflicts has been heralded by the Arab world as a victory, which begs the question, if they were all 'victories' how come Israel is still there? The only peace initiatives that were successful were with Egypt, under Sadat and Jordan under King Hussein. A golden opportunity was lost when, for years, Sadat and Hussein were sent to Coventry by the Arab world.

Over and over again they have been offered a settlement that would have gained them almost everything they demanded. The most generous offer from Israel came from Prime Minister Ehud Barak, at the Camp David summit in July 2000, with the backing of President Clinton. Prime Minister Barak, with President Clinton's support, offered 95 per cent of the West Bank, all of Gaza, a state with East Jerusalem as its capital and complete control of East Jerusalem, the Arab quarter and the Temple Mount.

To this they added $30 billion compensation for Palestinian refugees. Arafat rejected the package on the grounds that it did not include four million returning refugee families who had left in 1948, mainly at the urging of the Arab leadership who had attacked Israel confident that they could destroy her.

Could Israel have been more generous?

Could Israel have been more generous? They were not given the opportunity. Many Arabs were appalled at Arafat's rejection of this generous offer. Clinton and Barak had no doubt as to who was to blame, with Clinton repeatedly calling Arafat 'a liar'. The most scathing criticism, however, came from the Saudi Arabian diplomat to the UN, Prince Bandar, who described Arafat's rejection of the offer as 'a crime against the Palestinians – in fact against the entire region'. That was only part of the reason why Arafat rejected it. The real reason is because accepting it would have meant accepting Israel's existence, which Arafat would never do, no matter what was on the table.

Anyone who had any doubts about the standards of living enjoyed by the 22 Arab countries must have had their eyes opened by the daily coverage in the media of the *Arab Spring*. The nicest word to describe it is appalling. It has not been improved by the indiscriminate shelling of schools, hospitals, residential areas and basic infrastructure. How many billions this will cost the local Arab communities has not been calculated. Before the *Arab Spring*, figures quoted about the Arabs' standard of living suggest that the combined GDP of the Arabs' countries was less than that of Spain. And Spain, with an unemployment rate of 25 per cent, has hardly been an outstanding success.

Herein lies the tragedy of the Arab/Israeli conflict for the whole of the Middle East. The one country that could provide prosperity to the region is Israel. Despite its diminutive geographical size and population it has, largely through the influx of Jews from Europe and Russia, enabled Israel to become a leading nation in computer science, renewable and sustainable sources of energy, optics, medicine, agriculture, water management (it recycles 70 per cent of its waste water) military hardware and avionics. Israel enjoys one of the highest standards of living in the world. If it did not have to spend so much of its GDP on defence, the standard of living would be even higher. That is what Israel would love to be doing but not while the majority of the Arab world has as its only goal – the total destruction of Israel. Those who do not believe that Israel wants a genuine peace are living in a fantasy world.

Of course, not every Israeli agrees on what would be the best solution, but the Barak/Clinton plan is a good place to start. Which brings me back to the hard Left that have political control of the campuses of universities, colleges and many Left-wing political parties. They know how corrupt the Arab regimes are and how appalling the conditions are under which the majority of Arabs are forced to live. Imagine the standard of living if the Arabs did not have the oil that the rest of the world so desperately wants. Indeed, that may come to pass as a dramatic expansion of US production of oil and gas through 'fracking' technology could create excess supply and undermine the OPEC monopoly on oil prices.

Having sympathy for the plight of the Palestinians is a noble cause but pretending that the root cause of the corruption, poverty and illiteracy is the fault of Israel is ludicrous in the extreme. No country can improve the living standards of the Middle East better than Israel, but it cannot do it without the moral and physical support of the Left and the affluent Western countries that presently sit back, watch and do very little. They are prepared to accept Arab oil and the votes at international forums of the Islamic countries and their supporters to put pressure on Israel and none on the Arabs.

It is not difficult to understand why the Arab world and its supporters can almost always get the numbers at international forums to pass condemnatory resolutions regarding Israel. They can almost always count on at least three-quarters of the countries to support anti-Israel resolutions. Israel can only count on a handful of votes including the United States, Canada, Australia and a few of others. The Federal Government's recent decision to abstain from, rather than vote against, the UN vote to grant the Palestinian Authority observer status at the UN is a worrying sign. The Arab world and its fellow travellers show anti-Semitism at its worst.

3

Why the World Needs the Anglosphere

Peter Day

It hardly needs saying that Anglosphere countries have been responsible for many crimes and blunders. Indeed, many contemporary histories of the British Empire, from which the Anglosphere is ultimately derived, seem to consist of little else. It is the other side of the issue that tends to be ignored in school and university syllabuses, or even, against the evidence, denied. This is the side of the argument showing that the strongest predictor that a relatively poor country will transform itself into a relatively rich and broadly developed country is that it was a former British colony.

Better a British colony

Learned studies with elaborate statistical analyses prove the truth of this point. But they are hardly necessary. The most obvious, glaring example is of course the United States. Australia is another example, as are Canada and New Zealand. Hong Kong and Singapore are others that are especially pertinent, given their critical role as exemplars for the adoption of free market economic reforms that have transformed much of the Chinese mainland since Deng Xiaoping. Indian leaders also acknowledge that their country's striking economic development in recent years owes much to their nation's British legacy, including the political culture, educational system, wider institutional infrastructure and of course, most importantly, the English language.

My own favourite example of the benefits of Anglosphere membership comes not from such obvious cases, but from the ranks

13

of the smaller, tropical countries in regions where much of the world's poverty and political violence is to be found. The country I have in mind is the tiny, English-speaking Central American nation of Belize, whose population consists of just a few hundred thousand, mainly English-speaking Mayan Indians and the 'creole' descendants of African slaves, though more recently with a rapidly rising proportion of Hispanic-speaking refugees from neighbouring violence-torn Hispanic countries.

Previously called British Honduras, Belize adopted its name in the early 1970s on the way to achieving full independence from Britain in 1981. Its prospects at the time did not seem particularly bright and it remains today a poor country, with high unemployment and a rising crime rate, associated with the drug trade that inescapably pervades Central America and the Caribbean. But in its own context, it is not so poor. Its per capita GDP of around $8,500 is well above that of its coup-prone, dictatorial neighbours such as Honduras and Guatemala; and it also continues to boast much greater income equality across its population than it neighbours, as measured by the World Bank.

Most importantly, Belize has contrived to retain the institutional advantages for its people of a British legacy that includes a freely elected parliament, a free press, free expression, an independent judiciary, relatively low levels of corruption, a sound, compulsory education system, ethnic tolerance and a relatively open economy.

In its way, Belize has long been a regional bastion of stability, and a shining example to its neighbours of a possible path to peace and prosperity. But it only exists because of one other advantage: the provision of security by the UK. Only in very recent years has neighbouring Guatemala been prepared to recognise the sovereignty of Belize. The tensions are an unfortunate legacy of the Spanish empire in the region, which always refused to acknowledge the legitimacy of any English-speaking settlements on the 'Spanish Main'.

Thirty years ago, while roaming around Central America as a journalist, I once enjoyed a lunch in Belize with the commanding officer of a British SAS force there, including a contingent of Gurkhas and a couple of Harrier jump-jets tucked away under netting at the back of the Belize airport. Not many people seemed to know about these, but the Guatemalans certainly did. At that very time, the Guatemalan army was slaughtering its own country's Mayan Indians by the scores of thousands in multiple atrocities that are still matters of investigation under genocide hearings. The Guatemalans were also at that time doing little to disguise their deeply sanguinary intentions towards the Indians and blacks of Belize: all that was keeping them safe was that little British force. But that was then, in the time of Mrs Thatcher: the British force in Belize now has been sadly reduced to a risibly token effort.

It is certain that if richer Anglosphere countries do not protect the vulnerable smaller fry from predators, the predators will win. It is also certain that the budgetary crises now afflicting many Western countries will not be significantly helped by cutting expenditure on such efforts, since these budgetary crises are overwhelmingly caused not by defence spending but by exploding welfare 'entitlements'.

Lack of confidence and morale

A more important cause of the trend toward retrenchment in defence and international security spending seems to be a growing lack of confidence and morale among the policy-making elites, which seems to be related in turn to the capture of key areas of the educational system over the last 30 years by the generation of anti-Western ideologues who moved into the universities in the 1960s and 1970s, and who have been well-placed ever since to train the successor 'x' and 'y' generations now emerging into prominence.

There is certainly precious little underlying logic to the growing sense of pessimism. The tremendous advantages in institutional culture that have underpinned the relative success of the main Anglosphere countries for the past three centuries or so are also providing the platform for their likely continued material dominance for the foreseeable future.

This assertion of course goes against the grain of the overwhelming sense of decline that pervades much current commentary on the core Anglosphere nations, usually accompanied by somewhat over-excited predictions related to the forthcoming 'Asian century'. But recent empirical studies demonstrate clearly that it is precisely this fashion in current affairs commentary which is off-target.

One such study is the easily accessible, refreshingly fact-based presentation in the Winter 2012 issue of the US publication *City Journal*, co-authored by the distinguished urban studies scholar Joel Kotkin. The November/December 2012 issue of the influential journal *Foreign Affairs* carried a similarly devastating piece on the recently fashionable economic hyping of the so-called 'BRIC' countries (Brazil, Russia, India and China), in an exposé by the noted macro-economic writer and analyst Ruchir Sharma.

Kotkin and his co-author, business analyst Shashi Parulekar, name Australia as one of a group of just six core Anglosphere countries – the others being the US, the UK, Canada, New Zealand and Ireland – which together account for no less than a quarter of the world's entire GDP: around $US18 trillion. With per capita GDP of nearly $US45,000, no other group comes close to this – or has any realistic prospects of doing so. It is, for example, currently more than five times the per capita GDP of the so-called Sinosphere group consisting of China, Taiwan, Hong Kong and Macau.

In business, entertainment, science, technology and the arts, the flow-on effects of the overwhelming global ascendancy of the English language are vast. In Europe, more than twice as many people now speak English as those who speak French. English is also the preferred tongue in developing countries from West Africa to South-East Asia. This language ascendancy supports, for example, the Internet dominance by Anglosphere leviathans such as Amazon, Facebook, Microsoft, Google and Apple. It is also the platform for Anglosphere supremacy in movies, television, music, fashion and publishing (including scholarly publishing).

The same story holds good for aerospace, pharmaceuticals and a host of other industries where Anglosphere firms reign supreme.

It is necessary to point out that this data entirely supports the supposedly controversial claims made by Opposition leader Tony Abbott in his excellent July 2012 speech to the Heritage Foundation in Washington DC. Abbott's was in fact a carefully-balanced talk in which he freely conceded that the extent of American international dominance would not be as great in the future as it has been in the recent past. He also enthusiastically celebrated the great economic strides that have been made in Asia in recent times, especially by China and India. Alluding to the substantial (and not merely symbolic) initiatives of his conservative predecessors in strengthening ties with Asia, from Menzies through Holt, Fraser and Howard, he made clear his determination to follow their examples. But he argued that the facts simply did not support the conclusion now being drawn by many, that the US was passing from a dominant to a declining power. If the twenty-first century were going to be the Asian century, it would also be an American century.

Abbott could have made an even stronger case for the likelihood of continued American dominance, simply by referring to the looming demographic crises facing many non-Anglosphere countries including China, Japan and Russia, not to mention much of continental Europe. It was no doubt only the obvious requirements of tact and prudence that he chose not to do so. But if demography is fate, the message is clear: while population growth in Europe, Russia, China, Japan and elsewhere is declining or even turning negative, this is not the case in the Anglosphere. Australia's population has risen over the past 30 years or so by about 70 per cent; Canada's by nearly 100 per cent; New Zealand's by around 40 per cent and that of the United States by more than 30 per cent. Even the UK, for all its problems, is recording unprecedented immigration levels.

No Anglosphere country is perfect, but not many people leave them. To the contrary: people in flight from failing governance models elsewhere are voting with their feet for the traditional and successful Anglosphere model of political stability, rule of law, low levels of corruption, parliamentary government, ethnic and religious tolerance, free expression and property rights. This is predominantly why they are arriving in Australia, as they are arriving even in Belize.

But some of the commentary on Abbott's Washington speech provided a disturbing glimpse into the kinds of shortcomings that are now affecting the quality of public discussion about issues such as the Anglosphere. Abbott did not actually use the word 'Anglosphere' in his Washington speech, but even his brief and entirely proper discussion of the proud history of the English-speaking peoples was met with more or less openly sniggering commentary.

One important and particularly egregious example comes from the Lowy Institute. It was seriously disappointing to find the Institute's main Internet commentator, Sam Roggeveen, alleging in his analysis of Abbott's speech that his 'boasting on behalf of the English-speaking world reveals an uncertain grasp of history: and if you're Russian, a rather offensive one too. For, according to Abbott, Britain and her colonies 'stood alone' against Nazi Germany'. The statement of Abbott's here referred to by Roggeveen, about Britain and her colonies 'standing alone' against Nazi Germany, was perfectly correct. Yet this was the only specific statement offered by Roggeveen to justify his claim that Abbott possesses an 'uncertain' grasp of history.

Some lessons of history

In order to defend Abbott, it should not be necessary to have to reassert such basic historical facts as that Russia (then the Soviet Union) signed its infamous Non-Aggression Pact with Nazi Germany on 23 August 1939; and that this was the trigger for Nazi Germany's attack on Poland a little over a week later; and, that while Great Britain immediately declared war with Germany, the Russian dictator Stalin merely looked on benignly and maintained Russian neutrality.

Nor should it be necessary to recall that under the Pact between Hitler and Stalin, they had agreed that Poland would be divided between them, and that Russia would be given carte blanche to seize Latvia, Lithuania and Estonia as part of the carve-up of eastern Europe by the two gangster states. Nor that, as a consequence of the above, Great Britain and its empire, including Australia, did indeed stand alone against Nazi Germany for a period of nearly two years. Why on earth would Russians be offended? The period when Britain and the empire stood alone was only brought to an end by the surprise German invasion of its erstwhile Russian partner-in-crime, on 22 June 1941.

It needs to be said that the Lowy Institute's problem here is no more than the tiny tip of a very large iceberg. Anecdotal evidence suggests that the grievous shortcomings in our higher educational systems are already being felt in foreign policy-making, and even in the analysis of intelligence as graduates move up the bureaucratic food chain. The problem is not just graduates' low level of historical knowledge, but also the apparent failure of the graduates themselves to realise this. The obsession of universities and other institutes of higher learning with 'theory' seems to mean that they simply no longer impart historical knowledge as such, except incidentally. Thirty years ago, this was perhaps tolerable: it might then have been reasonable to assume that such knowledge had already been imparted at secondary school level. But no longer.

4

School Choice Matters to Poor Students

Kevin Donnelly

According to the Gonski Review of Funding for Schooling, one of the main reasons government students under-perform, compared with those attending non-government schools, is because they come from disadvantaged backgrounds. The belief that there is a strong correlation between disadvantage and failure is incorrect. Australian research carried out by Melbourne-based Gary Marks argues that socioeconomic background only accounts for between 9 and 16 per cent of the variance in educational outcomes across schools.

More important than home background in explaining why some students outperform others and why non-government schools, on the whole, achieve better results are factors such as student motivation and ability, classroom discipline and school culture, school leadership and the quality of the curriculum and teacher effectiveness.

Critics mistakenly argue that non-government schools are only successful – as measured by literacy and numeracy tests, Year 12 results and tertiary entry – because they enrol students from privileged backgrounds. The reason non-government schools outperform most government schools is not because their students are from wealthy backgrounds. Rather, it is because such schools are more successful at motivating students of every background.

Although there are many non-government schools serving affluent communities, it should also be remembered that the largest growth in non-government schools over the last 20 years-or-so has been in low fee-paying non-denominational schools serving low- and middle-class communities. Catholic systemic schools, largely parish based, also serve many communities throughout Australia that are characterised as disadvantaged because of high numbers of non-English speaking migrant students, aboriginal students and those from rural and remote regions.

Funding Myths

More than 34 per cent of students across Australia are enrolled in non-government schools. In the period 2000-2010, enrolments in non-government schools grew by 21 per cent, while enrolments in government schools grew by 1.1 per cent. While non-government school critics argue that such schools are over-funded by governments and over-resourced, the reality (based on 2010 Productivity Commission figures) is that students in such schools, on average, receive approximately half of what state school students receive in terms of recurrent funding.

State school students receive $14,300 while the equivalent figure for students attending non-government schools is $7,400. It is also the case that, unlike government schools which receive capital funding, non-government schools and their communities are responsible for land, buildings and infrastructure costs.

Catholic and independent schools are an essential part of Australia's tripartite system of education. This is primarily because, in addition to achieving strong educational outcomes and meeting the needs of a diverse range of families and communities, such schools save state and Commonwealth governments approximately $6 billion a year, the cost of teaching these students in the state system.

Notwithstanding their popularity and success, critics argue that non-government schools should not be funded and that the existing school socioeconomic status (SES) funding model is inequitable and socially unjust. The SES model was introduced by the Howard Government and is due to expire at the end of 2013. Best illustrated by the Gonski review of school funding commissioned in 2010 by Julia Gillard when education minister, related research papers and submissions from the Australian Education Union and like-minded academics, the belief is that Australia's education system is in urgent need of reform.

Critics argue that instead of promoting social mobility and fairness for all, the way in which schools are funded further disadvantages working class, migrant, Aboriginal and other so-called victim groups. They also argue that, whereas government schools are open to all on the basis that they are 'free, compulsory and secular' and have open enrolment practices, non-government schools discriminate in terms of who they enrol and are restricted only to those families that can afford to pay fees. Their solution to the alleged problem is to deny funding to Catholic and independent schools and to give priority to government schools serving disadvantaged communities.

This ignores the fact that the current SES funding model is based on need, a situation where wealthier non-government schools only receive a fraction of what government schools receive in terms of recurrent funding. Also ignored is the right which parents have to choose a school that best embodies the beliefs and values they consider important and not to be financially penalised because of school choice. Promoting the equity myth mirrors the more widespread belief that the cultural-Left must take the long march through the institutions – such as schools, universities and government bureaucracies – to ensure that society is transformed to make it conform to the utopian ideal where all achieve the same level of success.

In its more extreme form, the equity myth is also used to argue that academic subjects and competitive assessment are simply tools employed by society's elites to reinforce their privileged position and to disempower and marginalise those less fortunate. The flaws and weaknesses in the equity argument are manifest.

If accepted as true, the belief that working class, migrant and indigenous students are destined to under-perform because of their socioeconomic background represents a self-fulfilling prophecy that condemns such students to perpetual failure. It is also ironic that critics of non-government schools, committed as they are to supporting and promoting government schools, describe such schools as disadvantaged and residualised. As a result, they tarnish the reputation of such schools and make them less popular with parents.

Critics are wrong to characterise Australia as a land of inequality and entrenched disadvantage. Based on research carried out by the Organisation for Economic Cooperation and Development (OECD) Australia has a high degree of social mobility. Compared with other OECD countries, and in a large part due to our education system, children of any occupation and income are able to achieve more academically than their parents.

Australian society is not static and, as proven by the experience of many migrants who have settled in Australia over the last half century, there is a good chance that with effort, application and hard work families can improve their position in society. Based on the results of the Programme for International Student Assessment (PISA) tests, critics of non-government schools such as Barry McGaw, the head of the Australian Curriculum, Assessment and Reporting Authority (ACARA), argue that Australia's education system can be characterised by inequity because disadvantaged students are destined to underperform. This ignores the fact that an analysis of Australia's PISA test results over the last 10 to 12 years shows that there are occasions when our system can be characterised as high quality–high equity.

Research commissioned by the National Catholic Education Commission also concludes that Catholic schools, which enrol over 20 per cent of Australian students, are as successful as Finland, one of the world leaders in promoting excellence and helping at-risk students achieve much stronger than expected results.

Real Equity

Although rarely mentioned by critics of non-government schools, it is the case that there are many government schools in the eastern suburbs of cities such as Melbourne and Sydney that only serve wealthy communities and selective secondary schools that discriminate in relation to enrolments.

While critics argue that it is wrong for affluent parents to send their children to non-government schools, one wonders why the cultural-Left ignores the fact that only those who can afford million dollar real estate are in a position to buy property in the enrolment zones of sought-after government schools in better-off communities. Taken to its conclusion, the equity argument should mean that wealthy government school parents face some kind of financial penalty as do non-government schools parents.

It should also be noted that Catholic schools achieve stronger results than government schools, even though they receive less overall recurrent funding compared with state school students. Based on 2010 figures students in Catholic schools receive $9,679 per student, while governments school students are funded at $10,708.

There is an alternative to the equity myth and the cultural-left's politics of class envy. Research carried out by the German economist Ludger Woessmann concludes that a more market-driven approach to education leads to higher standards and increased equity. Stronger performing education systems are characterised by autonomy, diversity, competition and choice and a situation where non-government schools are properly funded and resourced.

If governments are genuinely concerned about strengthening educational outcomes, they should emulate the successful example of Australia's non-government schools, and better fund such schools to ensure that greater numbers of parents can afford school choice. As is occurring in the USA, one method to empower greater numbers of parents, especially those living in disadvantaged communities, is to introduce school vouchers. Simply put, every child should be entitled to a sum of money, with the possibility of an additional loading if required. Funding follows the child to the chosen school.

An alternative to vouchers is to allow tax credits for school fees and related costs. Both strategies are directed at removing the centralised, inflexible and bureaucratic nature of school funding in Australia. To be effective, school choice also depends on freeing schools, especially non-government schools, from provider capture. Instead of governments, education departments and teacher unions micro-managing and interfering in schools, schools should have the freedom to best reflect the needs and aspirations of their communities and, within general guidelines, to chart their own course.

Central in this regard is the need to respect the autonomy of non-government schools, what in the Catholic system is known as subsidiarity, and to allow government schools similar freedom and flexibility. All schools should be allowed to hire, dismiss and reward staff, manage their own budgets and set their own curriculum focus and school culture.

Unfortunately, based on the record of the ALP Commonwealth Government, under the leadership of both Kevin Rudd and Julia Gillard, the chances of such things happening are non-existent. Since being elected in 2007, firstly under the banner of Australia's 'education revolution' and now rebadged as a 'national crusade', the Commonwealth Government has embarked on a detailed and comprehensive strategy to wrest control of education from the states and to deny school autonomy.

Even though the national government neither manages schools nor employs teachers, all roads lead to Canberra. Initiatives include a national curriculum, national testing, national teacher registration and certification, making school data public on the MySchool website and tying compliance to funding.

In relation to the curriculum, the ALP Commonwealth Government is imposing a secular model that will force all schools, government and non-government, to teach every subject through a politically correct, cultural-Left prism involving Asian, environmental and indigenous perspectives. Of concern to faith-based schools is the fact that the history syllabus undermines Australia's Judeo-Christian heritage and the debt Australians owe to Western civilisation.

This ignores the fact that Australia is part of the Anglosphere (see the Peter Day chapter) and that its political and legal institutions and much of its history, language and culture can only be valued and appreciated in the light of the grand narrative associated with movements like the Glorious Revolution, the Renaissance, the Reformation and the Enlightenment.

The Gillard Government also defines the purpose of education and the work of schools as improving Australia's productivity and making the nation and its workers more internationally competitive in the so-called Asian century. This utilitarian view of education, with its primary focus on skills and generic competencies, represents a shallow, superficial and misleading view of education that undermines the search for truth and understanding – what Matthew Arnold termed, 'the best that has been thought and said'.

The Commonwealth Government is also increasing the amount of intrusive regulation and red-tape in education, under the guise of accountability and transparency, which will ensure that schools, especially non-government schools, lose their unique character and ability to manage themselves. The end game is to make it impossible to distinguish such schools from their government-controlled and managed counterparts by denying funding to Catholic and independent schools thereby destroying what makes them so popular and attractive to parents.

5

Science Matters in a Post-modern World

James Franklin

The muse of science

The ancients appointed Muses to look after history, dance, epic poetry and so on. There was even one for astronomy, which shows a breadth of view not always evident in today's arts crowd or law-trained ruling class. But there was not a muse for science, as we normally understand it – the sort with measurements, test tubes, graphs and theories.

Since we have the naming rights for the Muse of Science, let us call her Raelene. Rae's personality is a bit different from the others. She certainly delivers the goods, in the sense of stuff or cargo. Where Terpsichore (dance) and Calliope (epic poetry) are busy inspiring the higher Arts and finer feelings, Rae is at the shop table shovelling out the useful techniques and gaudy toys – medical breakthroughs, secret weapons, mobile phones, dental anaesthetics. A first reason why science matters is that it uncovers the principles on which technology is designed. The ideal place to recall the 'wonders of science' is sitting in the dentist's chair with the drill about to go in, so close to where the self is felt to be. It is good to know that the dentist's techniques and anaesthetics have been rigorously and scientifically tested. 'University tests prove' (as the ads say) that it is safe and will do you good.

So Rae is very generous, in an abstract kind of way. But she is also a touch autistic. She is ethically challenged, for one thing, in the way typified by Julian Assange (whose undergraduate studies were in physics and mathematics) who was more concerned with outing secrets than in wondering whether the effects would be good or evil. Victims of land mines and napalm are entitled to their vote that science sometimes has serious ill effects, and it is possible that a biology laboratory will yet come up with a micro-organism that eats us all. It is the nature of science that it delivers power without responsibility. It delivers power because it delivers knowledge. So science matters not only in a positive and benign sense, but in the sense that the tiger matters to him who is forced to ride it.

Science matters not only in its effects, but also in itself. It tells us what to think, and it does so without much respect for the wisdom of the elders. Polyhymnia, muse of sacred poetry, is on the side of tradition, and her followers are a docile and well-behaved, even conformist, lot. Rae, by contrast, is a bit of a troublemaker when it comes to the received ideas of the tribe. The sort of acolyte she prefers to inspire is a Galileo: forceful, troublesome, hard-headed, convinced of his own rightness (well, pig-headed, really), mathematical. If Rae has revealed that the earth moves, her disciples will be telling you that the earth moves, whether or not that is desirable, or useful, or aesthetically pleasing.

The truths which science delivers can be big ones. The Copernican Revolution showed that the Earth is not stationary in the centre of the universe, but a planet like others. Though it did not show, as Richard Dawkins claims, that 'We are insignificant creatures on a minor planet of a very average star in the outer suburbs of one of a hundred thousand million galaxies.' Science does not deal in that kind of 'significance', nor does it crassly judge moral importance by size or position. The Darwinian Revolution showed that our biology is the result of a continuous history of development going back four billion years. Though it did not show that humans are 'mere animals': it may be a surprising fact that humans share 99 per cent of their DNA with chimpanzees, but there is some reason why the chimps are not surprised by that, and cannot be surprised by that. The medical revolution of the late 19th and early 20th century doubled life expectancy. The Green Revolution around the 1960s made it possible to feed everyone easily. The computer revolution has been the main driver of change in their lifetime for most Westerners and the alternative scenario, global nuclear destruction, has been avoided. For the next generation, it may be biological enhancement. If you want significant facts, interesting facts, useful facts, believable facts, go to science.

But science matters not only by telling us what to think, but how to think. Science takes very seriously W.K. Clifford's austere and demanding principle of the ethics of belief: 'It is wrong always, everywhere, and for anyone to believe anything on insufficient evidence.' The reason why we can rely on what the dentist tells us about our fate over the next hour – though with less than 100 per cent certainty – is that there are logical relations holding between evidence and hypothesis. The evidence lies in the clinical trials that the dentist's materials and equipment have undergone, and in how the results of those trials bear on our case, for logical reasons.

Confirmation of theories by their consequences

The main idea is a simple but under-appreciated principle: the confirmation of theories by their consequences. If you have a theory and it predicts something that turns out to be true, then the theory is better supported (credible, confirmed…) than it was before. That is a principle not unique to science, though it is science that applies it with the greatest determination. The detective works out that if the butler did it, the knife is behind the sofa; the knife is found behind the sofa, so it is looking bad for the butler. Einstein predicts that if you go to West Africa you will see stars near the sun apparently shifted a little: that is how it is, so his theory of general relativity is confirmed. And that is not a matter of psychology, it is a matter of logic – what is really rational to believe: 'The verification of a consequence renders a hypothesis more probable.'

If very high probability is not enough, and one demands absolute certainty for at least the core of knowledge, then although empirical science cannot deliver that, mathematics can. No-one need accept tradition or experimental report in mathematics, because the truth is

plain for all to see (in simple enough cases, at least). Consider two rows
of three things, such as the ampersands below:

        &   &   &

        &   &   &

The brain provides us with a wonderful scientific visualisation facility,
or mind's eye (formerly called the imagination, before poets hijacked that
term). It allows us to mentally group objects in one way or another. We
can see the ampersands as two rows of three (2×3), or three columns
of two (3×2). Since they are the same objects, 2×3 must equal 3×2.
We not only know *that* $2 \times 3 = 3 \times 2$, we understand *why* it must be so.
Further, it is clear that there is nothing special about the numbers 2 and 3
and that the same argument would work for any larger rectangular array.
We understand why $n \times m$ must equal $m \times n$, for any numbers m and n, no
matter how large. That is a remarkable achievement: certain knowledge,
of an infinite number of truths, just by thinking. Plato's dictum 'Let
no-one ignorant of geometry enter here' summarised his view that the
guardians of the state should prepare their minds by contemplating the
truths of mathematics. It may be a plan worth reviving.

Of course, not everyone is happy about advances in rational
thinking, especially the academic enemies of rationality loosely called
'postmodernists'. In the more rarefied reaches of university humanities
faculties, it is *de rigueur* to describe science as 'socially constructed',
implying that its results do not depend on evidence but on the wishes of
the powerful. Postmodernists have been ridiculed, hoaxed, refuted and
voted against in appointments committees, but are still hanging on and
managing to appoint clones of themselves. The struggle continues.

The importance of the struggle for the rationality of science is
clear when we consider the historical and political effects of science,
sometimes not fully appreciated by some humanities-trained historians
and some political scientists. What caused the fall of the Soviet Empire?
Gorbachev's glasnost? The trio of Reagan, Thatcher and the Pope?

People's unquenchable desire for freedom? Soviet economic ineptitude? All of those things, certainly. But there was an equally important cause that had been undermining Soviet pretensions for some time, and came to a head in the 1980s. It was the glaring and growing gap between East and West in science and science-based technology, especially military technology. That had not always been the case – the launch of Sputnik in 1957 showed that the Soviets had a lead in some important areas in earlier years. But by the 1980s, as Western military and communications technology became computerised, the Soviet armed forces ossified. Fearing the openness that comes with interlinked computers, Soviet military and telecommunications facilities could not modernise. The repressive political system killed the flow of ideas needed for scientific progress. The imbalance between East and West started to show. In 1983, Reagan's Strategic Defense Initiative ('Star Wars') promised a computer-controlled system to intercept missiles. It may or may not have been technically feasible, but the Soviets knew they had no answer. The Chernobyl disaster of 1986 and the incompetent reaction to it showed up Soviet technology as inferior. Then in 1987 the 18-year-old Mathias Rust flew a Cessna through 800 kilometres of Soviet air defence and landed near Red Square. Heads rolled and the Soviet military looked a joke. Power that is not backed by consent is backed by force. Force is backed by military superiority. Military superiority is backed by technological superiority. If that is lost, and obviously lost, the whole pack of cards is ready to collapse.

Soviet ideology is not the only one with the potential to tangle with science and come off second best. A fascinating thing about nature is that it is not subject to political whim and rhetorical force. It stands as a 'reality check' on what we would prefer to think. As Galileo put it in his usual direct style, 'in natural sciences whose conclusions are true and necessary and have nothing to do with human will, one must take care not to place oneself in the defence of error; for here a thousand Demostheneses and a thousand Aristotles would be left in the lurch by every mediocre wit who happened to hit upon the truth for himself.' So, if a statistical study claims to show that different races have unequal intelligences, it can be replied to with queries about biases in the testing, but it cannot be defeated by cries that it would be too awful if that were true, nor by political organising. Stalin's support of Lysenko's mad biological theories could make them 'win', in the sense of leaving only their supporters unliquidated, but it could not make plants grow.

In our time, the climate change debate is a case in point. The year 1997 was a suddenly hotter year globally. The climate scientists who had been warning about global warming took that to be confirmation of their views and predicted that the global temperature would continue to increase. The entire Left of politics – previously best known for abusing science over its contribution to the 'military-industrial complex' – suddenly decided that science was a good thing after all and turned its well-honed bullying techniques on doubters, comparing 'climate denialists' to Holocaust deniers. According to the theory of the climate sceptics – strangely, almost all of them on the Right of politics – 1997 was an aberration, implying that the temperature should fall back to normal.

So what did nature do? Confounding both sides, the temperature has stayed flat at the high level for fifteen years, neither increasing beyond that level nor falling back to the average. An inconvenient truth, all round. We will see if Rae has the last laugh.

6

Religion Matters for Faith, Hope and Love

Ian Harper

Observing Australian society through the lens of the mass media, one gains the impression that religion is of marginal relevance to the life of the nation, let alone to the lives of individual Australians. While conservative media outlets appear to respect the contribution that traditional religious observance makes to social cohesion, so-called Progressive elements struggle to suppress a sneering tone that often borders on contempt. For example, recent reportage of sexual abuse, especially of children, within religious institutions, even though secular institutions are also implicated, barely masks a long-held suspicion of hypocrisy and malefaction within the church.

Yet the 2011 national census reveals that 68 per cent of Australians confess a religious affiliation, the overwhelming majority to one or more of the Christian denominations. To be sure, this proportion has steadily fallen since the 1960s, when nearly 90 per cent of Australians cited a religious affiliation on the census form. Since that time it has become anything but fashionable to reveal one's religious adherence in public, and respondents to the census can simply leave the question of religious affiliation unanswered. Still, a clear majority of Australians take this opportunity to claim religious affiliation rather than deny it, in a nation that many, including perhaps those same respondents, would hasten to describe as a secular democracy.

Australians tend to treat their religion as a private affair

This is less surprising than might appear at first glance because Australians tend to treat their religion as a private affair. It is not that Australians despise or ignore religion – although some almost certainly do – but that they generally prefer not to advertise their religious beliefs. Filling in the census form is one thing but going public with one's religious faith, let alone proselytising, is quite another.

Australians' ambivalence towards public religiosity was evident from the very outset of European settlement. Although Governor Phillip obeyed his orders to 'take such steps for the due celebration of publick (sic) worship as circumstances will permit', he did so with neither personal conviction nor enthusiasm. The colony's first minister of religion, the Reverend Richard Johnson, who had been appointed at the urging of William Wilberforce and Henry Thornton, lamented the poor attendance at public worship services by soldiers, settlers and convicts alike. The worldliness of Australian society and widespread lack of interest in religious observance (even while acknowledging religious affiliation) is hardly a recent development.

Australians seem especially leery of mixing religion and politics. With the polar extremes before them of the state-sponsored or 'established' church in England and strict church-state separation in the United States, the framers of the Australian Constitution opted for a minimalist model. Apart from a brief acknowledgement of the 'blessing of Almighty God' in the Preamble, the only other reference to religion is Section 116, where the Commonwealth is enjoined against making 'any law for establishing any religion, or for imposing any religious observance, or for prohibiting the free exercise of religion.' In addition, 'no religious test shall be required as a qualification for any office or public trust under the Commonwealth.'

Notwithstanding the highly specific nature of these requirements, some Australians react viscerally to anyone who expresses their religious convictions in public life. They see this as a violation of church-state separation 'as laid down in the Constitution'. To the contrary, barring from public office any citizen who professed religious belief, solely on account of that belief, would constitute a 'religious test' and expressly contravene Section 116 of the Constitution.

The Australian Constitution appears to envisage a secular state, that is, a state that is neutral towards religious observance, neither directing it nor prohibiting it, but also providing that public trust can be vested in citizens irrespective of their religious persuasion or lack thereof. Rather than mandating separation of church and state, in the sense that religious sentiment should be denied any role in determining matters of general public interest, the Constitution appears to affirm that the state has no business either requiring or obstructing religious observance and that religious affiliation is no obstacle to the fulfilment of a public trust or the duties of public office. The Constitution is otherwise silent on the role of religion or religious institutions in affairs of state or more generally in Australian public life.

Religious sentiment is clearly important to many Australians

This is all to the good because religious sentiment is clearly important to many Australians. Even if they consider it intensely private and personal, religion nevertheless shapes their outlook and aspirations. To this extent, religion must matter for Australian public life because, at the very least, these same citizens vote, and occasionally also offer themselves for election or are appointed to public office. In exercising their influence over public decision-making, whether directly or indirectly, Australians of religious conviction bring their views to bear – as do those of no religious persuasion and those who are actively anti-theistic. The Constitution provides for as much and, in so doing, undergirds the plurality of Australia's democracy, which is not secular in the sense of being free of religious influence, but rather neutral in respect of the state's official stance towards religious faith and observance.

In this light, those who would deny religious institutions and

individuals of religious conviction a voice in the public arena are seen for
what they are: intolerant and anti-democratic. What people make of the
pronouncements of religious authorities and individuals is, of course,
another matter. But within the self-same limits of tolerance, respect for
difference and common courtesy that apply to all public utterances, there
can be no case for censoring religious voices just because they speak out
of religious belief. Nor can there be a case for protecting those who
express their religious views from hearing contrary opinions in reply,
some of which will be hard for them to bear. All of this matters because
the interplay of competing views and sentiments within the public arena
is the stuff of robust democracy. Indeed, without it, as Friedrich von
Hayek pointed out, the open society is threatened and liberty itself is
compromised.

Religion matters in a democracy because some people's beliefs are
informed by a religious worldview, and what people believe influences
the way they vote and the support they lend to one policy platform rather
than another. Religion also matters because it shapes the way believers
live their lives, and the influence they exert on their families, communities
and workplaces. As Tom Frame explains in *Losing My Religion*, 'Because it
deals with matters of life and death, religion has centrality, primacy and
ultimacy in human lives, and exerts an abiding influence on individual
attitudes and actions.'

Australians may be worldly and pragmatic but they struggle with
questions of identity and purpose no less than other human beings both
past and present. Those who profess a religious faith turn to their beliefs
to understand who they are in relation to the created order and its Creator,
and what purpose their existence serves in an apparently vast universe.
From contemplation of these existential questions and systematic
religious instruction flow moral guidance on how to distinguish good
from evil and ethical imperatives on how to live one's life. Views differ
on whether religion is the only source of such moral and ethical guidance
but the great religions are remarkably consonant on these matters, even

as they differ on fundamental questions such as the nature of God and divine influence in human affairs.

What is common to all religions is transcendence of divine will over human affairs. A godless worldview is one in which the free exercise of human will is both the ultimate purpose of human existence and the standard by which human lives should be judged. Religion points beyond the human self to a purer, higher existence and frames human experience and aspiration within the notion of a proper relationship between the human and the divine. The nature of this relationship and its fulfilment differs from religion to religion but the notion that there is more to human life than self-actualisation is a common theme.

In short, religion directs people beyond themselves to ultimate ends that transcend their selfish needs and desires. In the Christian tradition, these ends are summarised by the author of the faith as the 'Two Great Commandments', namely, love God with all your heart, mind, soul and strength; and love your neighbour as yourself. Loving God is a matter of the will (although aided, mysteriously, by the intervention of God himself through the agency of the Holy Spirit) and shows itself in trusting God's provision and obedience to Jesus' moral teaching. Loving neighbours is a conscious seeking after the welfare of those whom God places within one's sphere of influence. The Parable of the Good Samaritan is a story Jesus told in response to the question, 'Who then is my neighbour?' The import of the story is that your neighbour is someone to whom you can render immediate assistance, whom others for various reasons cannot or will not assist, and who may well be a stranger or even someone repugnant to you.

The ethic of loving neighbours resonates with most Australians, even if few would acknowledge their willingness to put themselves out for others as having any religious foundation. This is an area where our cultural heritage is inseparable from its roots in Christian faith. Willingness to help others, especially in dire need or distress and at risk to one's own life, has marked true Christian faith since the very beginning. The self-sacrifice of Christians caring for the victims of plague in Ancient Rome confronted traditional pagan attitudes towards the afflicted and infirm, and was instrumental in the eventual conversion of Emperor Constantine. His successor, Julian, who sought in vain to disestablish Christianity as the imperial religion, expressed his frustration that Christians cared for the poor and needy among the pagans as well as their own flock. He exhorted pagans to do likewise without any hint of irony, much as modern-day New Atheists exhort their followers to out-do religious organisations in ministering to the global poor – with equally limited success, it would appear.

The New Atheists, like Emperor Julian before them, miss the fundamental point – religious conviction drives behaviour in ways that often defy worldly logic (for better and, in some cases, for worse, it must be said). It is no coincidence that Christian believers have been and continue to be associated with some of the greatest humanitarian interventions the world has known, including the relief of poverty and disease, and perhaps most famously the abolition of the slave trade. In Australia, the Roman Catholic Sisters of Charity are well known for establishing and operating hospitals and hospices in our major cities. Their motto sums up their motivation: *Caritas Christi Urget Nos* – 'Christ's love drives us on'. Without the mainspring of God's love for human beings in Christ, Christian charities would soon wind down.

Inspiration

Religion matters because it inspires people to think beyond the narrow confines of their own lives and daily tribulations to encompass a wider perspective. Indeed, public life itself, including respect for basic human rights, freedom of speech and the rule of law, has deep roots in Judeo-Christian religion. Those who would deny, diminish or suppress religious conviction knowingly or unknowingly put an axe to the foundations of Australia's most cherished institutions and endearing national character traits.

Religion matters because it is a well-spring of *faith* that there is more to this life than material comfort; of *hope* for a better future for oneself, one's children and grandchildren – in this world, not just the next; and of *love* for one's fellow human beings. Friedrich Nietzsche exulted in the emancipation of humanity from what he saw as the obscurantism and oppression of religious belief but nevertheless despaired that godless nihilism would condemn humankind to lives of triviality and narcissism. Understanding the role that religious belief plays in inspiring the lives of individual Australians as well as in nourishing the quality of our shared public life is essential to averting any descent into triviality and narcissism. Antagonism towards religion in public life and a wilful exclusion of religiously inspired views from the public square will surely speed us down a path in that direction.

7

Downsize Canberra: Remove Federal Income Tax

John Humphreys

Federal 'tax reform' generally means nothing much more than a slight change in marginal income tax rates and brackets, tweaking excise taxes or tax concessions, and occasional hushed murmurs about increasing the GST. None of these reforms effectively address the largest public finance problem facing Australia – that Canberra raises 80 per cent of revenue but spends around 50 per cent. The 'unspent' portion of money raised by Canberra is distributed to the states. This 'vertical fiscal imbalance' leads to low quality state government, ever more centralisation of political power in Canberra, and poor public policy.

Our broken system

The original idea for the Australian federation was sound, with states competing with each other to introduce better policies, and different states able to pursue different priorities, while the central government limited itself to core national issues such as trade and defence. However, the last hundred years has seen a steady shift of power to the centre so that the federation is now bastardised beyond recognition. The current mix is the worst of all worlds, with very little state-based diversity and competition, but a complicated system of pointless duplication and shifting blame.

While states retain the semblance of policy independence, their reliance on Canberra revenue means that they are now more like

43

dysfunctional arms of the federal bureaucracy, rather than independent jurisdictions able to experiment with new policy ideas. If a state introduces a productivity-enhancing reform, most of the extra revenue will go to the Federal Government and get shared with non-productive states. If a state introduces poor policy that harms its economy, other states are forced to help pay for the mistake. In other words, the current system subsidises state government mistakes and taxes their successes. This leads to lower quality state governments.

The dominant zeitgeist is for further centralisation of power with the all-knowing politicians and civil servants in Canberra. The Australian Labor Party has long promoted the centralisation of power, but more recently the conservative side, in particular John Howard and Tony Abbott, have also supported a 'Big Canberra' agenda. Compared with the current mess, it is easy to see why people would be attracted to the simple solution of Canberra control. But it is a false dichotomy to suggest that our choices are the broken status quo or a bigger federal government. The other option is to return to the intentions of the constitution, downsize Canberra, and re-create an effective federalism where states are free to pursue their goals, driven by competition to improve policy. However, this vision requires a fundamental re-think of tax.

Income tax reform

In order to fix the federation, federal income tax needs to be abolished. Meaningful tax reform in Australia should include removing the federal income tax, and once again allowing state-based income taxes. When Australia first became a nation, income tax was solely the domain of state governments. During WWI the Federal Government introduced a federal income tax, but in the following decades it remained a very small part of the tax system. It was only in 1942 that the Federal Government took over income tax from the states.

The rationale for a federal income tax is the same as the general argument for centralisation – that people do not want to deal with multiple rules in different parts of the country, and that the federal government can generally be trusted to do the right thing. It is certainly true that having state-based rules can create additional compliance costs for people who do business across state borders. However, this cost is often overstated. Further, the benefits of diversity and competition, although significant, are understated.

The benefits and costs of government competition are similar to the benefits and costs of business competition. Different producers sometimes behave quite differently, and consumers must deal with that diversity. However, this cost is more than offset by giving consumers a choice of different options and competitive pressures leading to better products at a lower cost.

Likewise with government competition, it is fairly easy to provide guidance for businesses so that they can easily comply with multiple rules, and these costs are more than offset by policy diversity and competition. If tax and spending policies are decentralised to the states and territories, then there will be eight times more opportunity for policy innovation, as well as greater incentives to copy successful policy and abandon failed policy. But these benefits of competitive federalism can only be achieved if states are responsible for raising their own revenue, so the vital first step in fixing federation is to return to the states the power to tax income.

In exchange for income taxing powers, the states would give up the 'general purpose payments' that the federal government distributes each year, meaning that they would no longer be reliant on handouts from Canberra and would once again control their own revenue. An additional benefit of this change is that it would allow for the merging of the state income taxes with state payroll taxes to create a more streamlined, transparent and efficient tax system.

Not only would states become financially independent, this reform would significantly increase state revenue. For 2012-13, income tax is estimated to raise $164 billion while state grants are estimated to be about $49 billion, so a state income tax would increase total state revenues by

$115 billion. Because such reform could not be implemented immediately, the remainder of this article will consider the financial consequences of the proposed reforms assuming that the changes are complete for 2015-16, at which time the extra state revenue will be about $150 billion per year. That means the tax revenue going to the states will approximately triple, rising from just over 4 per cent to 12.5 per cent of GDP. With this extra revenue, states could take back responsibility for some areas of spending that had previously been passed to Canberra.

In contrast, federal government revenue will decrease from an estimated $438 billion (24.2 per cent of GDP) to $288 billion (15.9 per cent of GDP). This is still more than enough to cover core federal responsibilities, while other areas of spending can be handed over to the states. If it was decided that more revenue needed to be decentralised, that could easily be achieved by lowering – or abolishing – the federal company tax, which would allow more income to be caught in the income tax system and therefore increase state income tax revenue. But that is a topic for another time.

One immediate objection is that the states do not have the necessary administrative systems to run an income taxation system. The simple solution is that state income taxes could continue to be coordinated by the Australian Tax Office, which would be working on behalf of state governments.

A second objection to this reform is that some states will raise more revenue than others, and the federal government may want to take money from the more productive states to subsidise the less efficient states. While such a system creates warped incentives, if the federal government does want to achieve inter-state redistribution they are still free to do that explicitly by directly taking from 'rich' states and subsidising 'poor' states. Indeed, instead of being hidden inside other tax arrangements, it is preferable that such redistribution should happen transparently so that it can be judged on its merits.

Returning responsibilities to the states

The last piece of the puzzle is to work out which areas of spending should be decentralised to the states. The most obvious options are the areas that currently have a significant amount of duplication between state and federal levels of government – primarily, health and education. Health and education are also policy areas in need of more policy innovation and reform, which is more likely under proper competitive federalism. Although the Australian economy has undergone important microeconomic reform in many areas over the past few decades, these reforms have not extended to health and education. One of the reasons is that the split responsibility between federal and state governments has made change almost impossible.

Currently, the Federal Government funds private schools while the state governments fund public schools. Many reform ideas – such as a comprehensive student-based funding model – are not possible in such an environment. In the current health system, state governments run the hospitals while the Federal Government funds operations, doctor visits and pharmaceuticals. The split responsibilities lead to poor policy and blame shifting, while any serious attempt at reform is prevented because nobody has ultimate responsibility.

Health in particular is in need of policy innovation. The government's Intergenerational Report (IGR) clearly shows that government spending on health and aged care is unsustainable. By the middle of this century, government spending will need to increase by about 5 per cent of GDP in order to maintain the current systems. This increase is the equivalent of tripling the GST, or doubling income tax rates (without any extra benefits). It is exactly this sort of budget pressure that has led Europe and America to the brink of financial collapse. Australia needs to start looking at health policy solutions as soon as possible if it wants to ensure fiscal sustainability. By shifting all health responsibilities to the state level, not only will reform become possible, but there will also be eight jurisdictions competing to discover better policies.

Using the estimates for 2015-16, the federal health budget is $71 billion (including $3.3 billion in administration) and the federal education budget is $34 billion ($0.3 billion in administration). Combined, this comes to $105 billion that could be transferred from Canberra to the states. If the Federal Government kept responsibility for aboriginal health issues, then this would drop to $104 billion. It is also possible that the states would be able to find some savings by reducing administrative duplication.

Given that the states are receiving an additional $150 billion, it is possible to decentralise even more government spending. One option would be to decentralise transfer payments that are closely linked with the income tax system, allowing the same authority to be able to manage the vexed issue of high 'effective marginal tax rates'. For 2015-16, total family payments are estimated to be $37 billion while unemployment assistance is expected to cost just under $10 billion, which comes to a total of $47 billion in non-pension transfer payments. If this spending, along with health and education, were transferred to the states, then the spending shift would almost perfectly match the suggested revenue shift.

Looking forward

It is fairly easy to make the case that the current system is a broken combination of the worst elements of federalism combined with the worst elements of centralisation. Change is needed. Many academics and politicians have written about the benefits of competitive federalism, but without the decentralisation of income tax (and health/education spending) to the states, the supposed benefits cannot be achieved. With this reform, the federation can start to work as it was intended. Without this reform, it is nearly impossible to see how Australia can escape from the current approach of duplication, blame-shifting, policy sclerosis, and an ever-growing Canberra bureaucracy.

Although removing the federal income tax and shifting more tax and spending powers to the states may seem radical at first, it is actually the most pragmatic solution to current problems. Any other response will require the agreement of many different governments with competing interests or constitutional amendments, both of which are extremely difficult. In contrast, the solution suggested here can be done with a simple majority of the federal parliament.

If the Federal Government stopped funding the states, and instead offered states the use of the ATO to co-ordinate their state income taxes, the transition would be quite straightforward. There is good reason to be optimistic about the results. By ensuring states are responsible for their own revenue, states will have incentives to be more productive and efficient. By ensuring that states have total control over health and education, reform not only becomes possible, but eight times more likely.

8

European Union as Self-aggrandisement

Michael James

Absence of euro scepticism

Since the Roman Empire collapsed in the fifth century, Europe has undergone several cycles of centralisation and disintegration. In the last two centuries alone it has experienced two complete such cycles, as the short-lived continental empires of Napoleon and Hitler were destroyed by the wars they occasioned. The European Union (EU), which emerged after WWII, is the first attempt in modern times to unite Europe by peaceful means. The present, seemingly permanent economic crisis of the Eurozone (which embraces 17 of the EU's 27 members) may yet initiate another phase of disintegration, if the apparent determination of Europe's political elites to save the euro at all costs backfires by provoking the defection of bankrupt member states such as Greece and Portugal. Yet what is truly remarkable about the crisis is the absence in the worst-affected states of any serious political movement to exit either the Eurozone or the EU itself. While the Greek people bitterly resent the extreme austerity imposed on them by the EU in exchange for bailouts, they want to stay with the euro. That preference is reflected at the top: in the entire Eurozone, not a single mainstream political party has so far questioned the EU's commitment to the euro, even though it is becoming ever clearer that the euro is itself a major cause of Europe's economic stagnation and long-term decline.

Against this background, the EU's ambition to convert the Eurozone into a full economic and even political union may yet be realised. But the price of that union would be a loss of national sovereignty and of democracy itself, even if these were willingly surrendered by the present voting generations. Democracy requires a 'demos', a community that spontaneously shares a common destiny and confers legitimacy and authority on the decisions of its political agents. But the EU has no such demos. The apparatus of the EU is carefully designed to give the impression that a European demos exists: it includes a parliament elected by universal adult suffrage, an executive headed by a 'president' (though unelected), a court, a central bank, a currency, and even foreign embassies, a flag and an anthem. But no-one is fooled. When Germany was reunified in 1991, West Germans were reluctant enough to bail out even their impoverished fellow-Germans in the East. The Germans' resentment at being made to finance the lion's share of the EU bailout of Greece, with its widespread institutionalised corruption and absurdly overblown and cosseted public sector, is naturally far greater. But their grudging acquiescence in the bailout is no indication of an underlying 'democratic' identification with fellow-Europeans. Rather, it reflects the decision Germany made after WWII – in the circumstances, the only choice it could make – to coexist and cooperate peacefully with its neighbours. Faced with the long-term consequences of that choice, it now finds itself forced to promote economic and political union – crucially including direct EU control of member states' budgets – as the only way to avoid going bankrupt itself in the effort to keep the Eurozone afloat.

Threadbare peace rationale

This brings us to the underlying motivation and rationale of the EU. While each member state has had its special reasons for joining the EU, the initial impetus behind the drive to the 'ever closer union' enshrined in the EU's foundation Treaty of Rome (1958) was the ruinous legacy in Europe of two world wars and the overwhelming need to avoid further armed conflict, especially between France and Germany. The official

story is that the world wars had been caused by nationalism and that
the European peace since 1945 vindicates the creation of the EU. That
story is not quite as self-evidently true as it may seem. It is certainly the
case that the close post-war cooperation between France and Germany,
institutionalised initially in the European Iron and Steel Community set
up in 1951, was designed to solve the 'German problem' for both France
and Germany: France had a big, potentially aggressive neighbour it could
never subdue militarily, while Germany, which in 1933 had thrown away
a democratic constitution in favour of tyranny, was uncertain whether
it could trust itself not to do so again. Yet WWII had arguably been
caused not by nationalism but by ideology: the world had actually been
quietly sympathetic towards Germany's goal of restoring its national
unity after WWI, but then found that the Nazis were driven by a quest
for world domination based on a doctrine of Aryan racial supremacy.
After WWII the threat to world peace again came from an ideology, this
time communism; and the European peace arguably depended more on
NATO (an intergovernmental rather than a supranational organisation)
and the presence of US armed forces than on the EU. Meanwhile
democracy was universally embraced in Germany and became entrenched
there; this too would have bolstered the post-war European peace. The
EU could be plausibly interpreted as an effect of European peace as well
as, or instead of, a cause of it.

The more recent expansion of the EU has been driven by different
considerations. In the 1980s Greece, Spain and Portugal joined the
EU as a way of seeking recognition of their transitions from military
dictatorships to democracies. After the turn of the present century the
ex-communist countries of Eastern Europe joined, likewise seeking the
sanction of a democratic club but also hoping to balance the influence
of their big Russian neighbour to the east. More significant, however,
has been the steady growth of the power of the EU's institutions at
the expense of the member states, a shift of which the adoption of the
euro – managed by the supranational European Central Bank – in 1999

is the most momentous and visible example. But the anti-democratic tendencies of the EU were revealed unambiguously in 2005, when the EU neutralised the results of referendums in France and the Netherlands rejecting a proposed new EU constitution by renaming the constitution a 'treaty' so that most national legislatures could endorse it without having to put it to a popular vote. (Ireland did hold a referendum on the Treaty of Lisbon but, as the result was a 'no', a year later it held a second ballot that came up with the correct answer. In referendums in the EU, only when countries vote 'no' are they allowed the luxury of second thoughts.) Even more revealingly, in late 2011 the French and the German governments, determined to save the euro from collapse, secured the resignation and replacement of the heads of government of Greece and Italy virtually overnight. They displayed a ruthless and peremptory high-handedness for which they were not in the least apologetic or contrite, even though their conduct was reminiscent of the sort of international bullying in Europe's past that the EU was supposed to have made impossible.

As the powers of the EU have grown so have the size, remuneration and perquisites of its bureaucracy. And when a country joins the EU, it immediately acquires a powerful vested interest in favour of continued membership in the form of a cadre of Members of the European Parliament, commissioners and other officials who enjoy large tax-free salaries and access to generous and unaudited expense accounts. So embedded is the corruption in the EU that the auditors have declined to sign its books every year since 1994. The traditional response of the EU has been to seek higher contributions from the member states, even in 2012 when it was imposing austerity on several of them.

These horrors might be considered tolerable if they were a necessary price to pay for the maintenance of peace in Europe. But as we have seen, it is far from self-evident that the EU has been crucial to the European peace since 1945. Moreover, no other region of the world seems interested in adopting the model of supranational government that the EU would like to export. On the contrary, the sovereign nation state is going from strength to strength. The number of independent nation states rose considerably when communism collapsed and the Soviet Union dissolved; and it shows no signs of diminishing. The most dynamic emerging regions of the world – Asia and Latin America – have regional intergovernmental associations and free-trade agreements, but these do not compromise the sovereignty of their members. If any region of the world needs to adopt models that have succeeded elsewhere, it is surely Europe.

Self-aggrandisement

The European Union is thus best understood as a supranational power system devoted exclusively to self-aggrandisement, perhaps all the more so since its original justification is so threadbare. Its commitment to maintaining the euro is rational because the tensions between the EU and its member states are so great that the defection of a single member of the Eurozone could trigger the disintegration of the entire union. This is not to suggest that any such disintegration is imminent or likely. At present, the only member state in which the option of leaving the EU is openly discussed is the United Kingdom, which is not a member of the Eurozone. On one measure, more than half of the legislation that passes through Britain's parliament is in effect rubber-stamped without debate because it is initiated in Brussels: a fact that is widely resented. Meanwhile, in continental Europe the widespread disgruntlement about the EU stems not so much from derogations from national sovereignty as such; rather, surplus members of the Eurozone resent being made to bail out deficit countries, while the deficit members resent having to endure austerity in exchange for the bailouts. But the absence so far of any serious popular pressure to dissolve or even reform the Eurozone suggests a reversion to a resigned deference towards elite statecraft that predates the arrival of democracy. And it is worth remembering how recent the arrival of democracy is in much of Europe.

Yet the economic problems of Europe are so great (they flow not just from the euro but also from each country's unsustainably generous state welfare system) that the EU is bound to react to them either by continuing to attract power to the centre or by starting to devolve power back to the member states. There are some factors making for the latter possibility. The Eurozone could prove ultimately too expensive or too unpopular to sustain in its present form; some countries might renounce the euro and revive their old currencies, giving them the option of devaluing their way to recovery. In the next few years the United Kingdom may either quit the EU or negotiate some new and looser relationship with it; such a change would set a precedent that other member states might want to follow. And, as we saw with the Soviet Union, empires that have lost their *raison d'être* can unravel unexpectedly, suddenly and rapidly.

Against that, the EU elite has become expert in monopolising power, in turning the unimaginable into reality, and in neutralising opposition to it within member states. Its determination to make the euro work is absolute. In this it is supported by – indeed it overlaps with – the political elites of France and Germany, the two indispensable members of the EU. It would therefore be prudent to assume that the drive to turn the Eurozone into a full economic and political union – correctly presented as necessary to ensure the survival of the euro – will succeed.

Critics of the EU might seek comfort from adopting the longest possible perspective, and reminding themselves that, as noted at the start, all previous attempts to unite Europe from the top down have eventually succumbed to decentralising forces. But rather than relying on a dubious cyclical theory of history, the critics might instead stress that a Europe of independent sovereign nation states would be a happier place than the Europe of today. Indeed, a Europe whose peoples cooperated peacefully through trade, investment, migration and tourism, while each retained the sovereign right to determine the scope and limits of any further cooperation, would be realising what were once assumed to be the goals of the European Union. The ultimate complaint against the supranational monster that the EU has become is not that it is overbearing, or illegitimate, or wasteful, or corrupt, but that it is unnecessary.

9

Abolish the Human Rights Commission

Gary Johns

Who needs a human rights commission?

In January 2013, a federal magistrate found that the New South Wales Rail Corporation discriminated against blind and vision-impaired people because it failed to provide audible announcements on trains. Graeme Innes, the Federal Disability Discrimination Commissioner, commenced the action against Rail Corp. He did so as a private citizen. There were financial risks associated with the action, risks that would act as a barrier to others, but the law was clear and Innes, private citizen, won. Innes could easily have made the issue a lively segment on television current affairs, or indeed telephoned the state minister for transport. Each of these actions would probably have netted a 'victory'. The victory begs the question, why a Human Rights Commission?

Big breakthroughs in human rights in Australia had already been well and truly achieved by the time professionals had taken their positions in the Australian Human Rights Commission (AHRC), its predecessor and its state equivalents. (And other, smaller breakthroughs like Innes' are being achieved despite the Commission.) Citizens working within the liberal democratic polity had undertaken the hard work of change. Women had begun their long march into the workforce well before the *Sex Discrimination Act 1984*, which the AHRC administers. Migrants had begun to integrate soon after WWII, well before the *Racial Discrimination Act 1975*, which the AHRC also administers. Aborigines have grown in stature and surety, but most of the work took place in the political realm.

Indeed, the *Racial Discrimination Act* has, arguably, become an instrument of discrimination inhibiting the further advancement of Aborigines. Nevertheless, the various discrimination Acts are not of themselves necessarily objectionable. The Acts grant litigants standing at court, and test cases, an eager media, and alert politicians are the stuff to change culture. The AHRC, however, is not. It is redundant. To make itself less so it celebrates slight and offence, not blatant discrimination. The AHRC and its acolytes have now deemed that which concerned citizens once imagined as reasonable debate, or soundly based differences in outcomes, beyond the pale.

The work of the AHRC demonstrates mission creep. Much of its work relates to allegations of workplace discrimination: it could be done by Fair Work Australia. The AHRC focuses on subjects as generic as bullying and domestic violence. It lobbies for resources for aged care, for employers to take on responsibilities unrelated to their business, for the National Disability Insurance Scheme, the removal of taxation on native title earnings, Aboriginal recognition in the Constitution, a Bill of Rights, and a decidedly anti-free speech consolidation of the Acts it administers. These are highly political matters and should not be the preserve of public servants. At $32 million per year (total cash received 2012) the work of the AHRC is not cheap. The fact that the AHRC proudly boasts that women comprise 73 per cent of the staff of the Commission suggests that it consists of true believers, not objective analysts.

The number of Commissioners continues to grow as the remit expands, recommended, of course, by the Commission. It is a mystery as to why there is an Aboriginal and Torres Strait Islander Commissioner in addition to a Race Commissioner. In addition to the Age Commissioner there is an Aged Care Commissioner working in conjunction with the AHRC. A Children's Commissioner is soon to be appointed. There is, separate from the AHRC, a Federal Privacy Commissioner. There is a Disability Discrimination Commissioner to administer the *Disability Discrimination Act 1992*. The Commissioner and the Commission have wildly exceeded their brief, however, by advocating the National Disability Insurance Scheme (NDIS). The NDIS has nothing to do with discrimination. It is a resource issue that depends on the amount of money that taxpayers are prepared to pay to make the life of the disabled more comfortable. The AHRC may have framed the issue as a human right, but who the disabled are, how much they should receive and how money is to be raised are questions that only citizens, through elected representatives can, and should, decide.

Real change

A prime example of how women and non-Anglo Celts have managed to overcome prejudice, before the Commission's establishment, is their success in the workplace and in society. For Aborigines, the rate of intermarriage indicates lack of prejudice among non-Aborigines towards Aborigines. The proportion of indigenous couple families with one partner not indigenous (in major urban areas) was 75 per cent in 1986, which suggests that a high level of integration had been applying before the establishment of the AHRC. The rate of intermarriage in rural areas was only 30 per cent in 1986, which suggests that propinquity and opportunity were probably the powerful determinants of intermarriage, not an AHRC 'program'. The same applies to employment, which for Aborigines is highest in major centres and lowest in remote areas, the reverse for non-Aborigines. It appears that the AHRC, and probably the Act, are irrelevant to the Aboriginal journey.

For women the world has changed. During the post-WWII baby boom relatively few women were employed (and of those employed relatively few were married). In 1954, 29 per cent of women aged 15-64 in Australia were employed (and only 31 per cent of these women were married). At that time, married women were generally expected to support the family at home, while their partners were the breadwinners. In 1983, 45 per cent of women aged 15-64 in Australia were employed. By 2005, the numbers had risen to 57 per cent. No change can be attributed to the AHRC before 1984. How much could be attributed to the post-1984 changes?

George Friedman (*The Next 100 Years*) writes 'A woman will live twice as long as her ancestors and will for over half her life be incapable of reproduction ... Time exclusively devoted to having and raising children will be reduced to an astounding 10 per cent of her life.' In Australia, in 1934 the total fertility rate was 2.1; births to a woman of five or more constituted nearly 18 per cent of all births and the median age of mothers at first nuptial birth was 24.4 years. In 1996 the respective figures were 1.8, 2.3 per cent and 28.7 years. As in many other countries, the levels and patterns of women's participation in work have undergone substantial change because the time devoted to raising children has shrunk dramatically. Other real drivers were changes in work processes, which created more non-manual jobs, and the growth of service industries.

On the policy side, the drivers were likely to have been direct measures such as the removal of the marriage bar from employment in the Commonwealth Public Service in 1966, and in the states at various times, and the ruling of the Commonwealth Conciliation and Arbitration Commission in 1969 that women should receive equal pay to men for equal work. A 2003 study (Jaumotte, *OECD Economic Studies*) examined the determinants of female workforce participation – with a particular focus on married women – in 17 OECD countries (including Australia) over the period 1985 to 1999. It found the following policies had a positive influence on female participation:

- Neutral tax treatment of second income earners relative to single earners.
- Childcare subsidies.
- Paid maternity and parental leave.

To these may be added female education, well-functioning labour markets and cultural attitudes. The *Sex Discrimination Act* in 1984, and the

Affirmative Action (Equal Employment Opportunity for Women) Act in 1986 may have played a part in accentuating a trend in women's participation in the workforce, but the key drivers: demographic, direct hiring practices, taxation and labour market matters are not in the remit of the AHRC.

The case for distinguishing underlying real causes of change and after-the-fact proselytising, may be also drawn for migrants. The Australian Bureau of Statistics' *Survey of Employment and Unemployment Patterns* is a longitudinal survey in which the same individuals are interviewed over a number of years. The 1995 survey shows that migrant jobseekers who were born in predominantly non-English speaking countries but spoke English very well had greater success in finding employment at some stage after May 1995 (60 per cent found employment) than those who said they did not speak English well or at all (32 per cent found employment). Employer-nominated migrants and business-skills migrants had the lowest unemployment rate, and new humanitarian migrants had the highest unemployment rate (81 per cent among migrants who had been resident in Australia for about five months). These differences suggest that race discrimination is not the issue, but employability. Again, these are matters not in the remit of the AHRC. They have little to do with human rights, and everything to do with the reasonable requirements of employers.

Commission makes work

The AHRC keeps itself in business in a number of ways, but the key means are to broaden its mandate by lobbying to change the law. It seeks to broaden the definition of the offended; broaden the definition of an offence; intensify the offence; and degrade the defences available to the alleged offender.

At present, there are 18 'protected attributes', or types, who can claim discrimination. The 'protected ones' range from the usual – age, race and so on – to some more exotic, such as social origin, breastfeeding, political opinion and potential pregnancy. It works closely with lobbies in the human rights industry to suggest new ways to have government intervene in daily life, especially against employers. There are lobbies in the industry that want to expand the attributes to such people as those with 'cognitive diversity', homelessness, welfare recipients, compensation recipients and survivors of domestic or family violence.

Until very recently, the Attorney-General was seeking to broaden the definition of an offence in the new proposed consolidated Act. For the first time, discrimination (not just confined to racial hatred) would be defined to include 'conduct that offends, insults or intimidates' another person. Fortunately, James Spigelman, chairman of the ABC and former Chief Justice of the NSW Supreme Court, invited by the Human Rights Commission to deliver The Human Rights Day Oration, addressed the question. He concluded: 'The freedom to offend is an integral component of freedom of speech. There is no right not to be offended.' Having tasted success by 'silencing' Andrew Bolt for blowing the whistle over alleged privileged white Aborigines, the human rights industry thought it should emulate that success across all attributes.

Intensifying the offence is also a good move for the AHRC. It leads to exquisite wording, sure to entrap many potential offenders. For example, one can be found to have sexually harassed another person if one failed to 'anticipate the possibility that the other person would be offended by the first person's conduct'. Degrading the defence of the alleged offender is also getting a run in the new draft laws. For example, a case study presented to the Attorney-General's Department by the Aboriginal and Torres Strait Islander Women's Legal and Advocacy Service is instructive. An Aboriginal grandmother complained that the Department of Communities had cancelled her kinship-carer status and removed her grandchildren from her care. The reason given was that she had allowed her husband and others with a criminal history into her home. Police were regularly in attendance. The complaint? The reassessment of her kinship-carer status had been completed by a non-Aboriginal social worker.

The facts

Just how bad is discrimination in Australia that new and exotic grounds should be introduced? The AHRC's latest annual report records that in 2011-12 it received 2,610 complaints. There were 965 disability complaints, 502 sex discrimination complaints and a similar number under the *Racial Discrimination Act* and the *Australian Human Rights Commission Act*. The big growth business is under the AHRCA, particularly under the International Covenant on Civil and Political Rights. These are matters concerning the length or conditions of immigration detention, as well as complaints that detention or visa decisions constitute an arbitrary interference with the family. Only 208 complaints were lodged under the *Age Discrimination Act*, but give us baby boomers time. This is how the 2,600 complaints were dealt with. More than 800 were 'terminated/declined' and 547 were 'withdrawn or discontinued'. The remaining 1,200 were conciliated. In other words, in a population of almost 23 million (and taking into account there are state anti-discrimination commissions), fewer than 1,200 were actual complaints. Further, some unreported number may have been trivial, in that they may not have amounted to much, or ended in an admission of guilt.

The AHRC was an afterthought. It was a triumphal decoration hoist as a sign of domination among Progressives. But the key processes were already well under way long before the Commission came into being. Like all bureaucracies, their main work has been to convince government of their worth by expanding their brief and exaggerating the state of affairs. The AHRC has outstayed its welcome. It should be abolished.

10

Biodiversity Does Not Matter: Revealed Biodiversity Matters

Eric L. Jones

Biodiversity matters, or so we are told on every hand. At least, the 'environmentally worried elite' keep saying so. They seem to be reacting against what they think is the complete history of the natural world – a saga of endless battering and chopping into bits by our predecessors, followed by being rushed ever faster to hell in a handcart. Exploiting the world's biological resources has been wrong, and is wrong, the assertions go, if by doing so the 'natural' landscape is damaged or the population of any species is diminished. Nothing will be left for our children to enjoy, assuming that there will be anything for them to eat once we have despoiled the Earth and left it bare of everything except weeds, rats and cockroaches. The media go along eagerly with this doom-mongering – their patron saint is Chicken Little. They are rather good at tucking away on the inside pages any least hint of good news.

Dismal worldview

The consequences of soaking a whole generation in this dismal worldview are unfortunate. If everyone accepts that the planet is doomed, there is little point in building positive policies that might stave off its fate. But conservation bureaucrats and activists do not really want us to believe their own story. They want us to resist it, by supporting their demands that governments restrict the consumption of natural resources. They fail to grasp the power of substitution by trade or technology. They want us to spend more and more tax money on conservation, which means locking up ever larger areas of the bush and keeping them away from development, whatever the cost to society, or rather whatever the cost to people poorer than middle-class activists. Motherhood and apple pie require us to go along with these prescriptions for saving something from the wreck of human ambition. What is to be saved is above all the absolute maximum number of biological species, regardless of the difficulties of defining a species. Everything is to be saved, however much it costs to build a giant governmental ark. Biodiversity is sacrosanct, this much we are told. The moral imperative is to preserve it.

But biodiversity does not matter. Laments about the subject always ignore the other side of the equation. In fretting about the losses of birds, animals and plants, all sight is lost of the gains that have come from actually using natural resources. These gains have been astounding for a century or two, depending on which country is discussed. Consider: the human population has expanded, life expectancy has risen, the standard of living has gone up, and (amazingly enough) all at the same time. Should we choose this moment to halt human advance, to hold back on the economic growth that has achieved so much? Society always has more needs than it has the means to satisfy and in many less-developed countries the needs are beyond urgent, they are desperate.

Only people-haters could insist that economic growth in the poor countries is not a desirable goal, whatever the cost in creepy-crawlies or to the remoter reaches of the natural world. In any case the rate at which other organisms are becoming extinct is so grossly exaggerated that one wonders how anyone scientifically trained could have come up with it. Standing back and viewing the situation overall, wildlife can be seen to have adapted remarkably well to the human occupation of the Earth.

Admittedly, to state a case along these lines gets one a bad name. Showing a preference for humans is called speciesism. Yet anyone who would save the yellow fever bacillus from extinction at the risk of human babies had better put up a good argument. If this seems a cheap shot, it is not: we cannot resolve every problem simultaneously and it is ludicrous to think any society has the resources to do so. Moreover, no-one has shown just where the line should be drawn. Is all life sacred? Should we strain to preserve absolutely each and every species, whatever the cost? Are no distinctions to be drawn, and is no-one prepared to make a judgement – judgements are always being made by default, so this needs to be an open one – as to the mix of species that might be a feasible goal?

At the purely scientific level, Robert May (a Sydney physicist who became chief scientific advisor to the UK government) has shown that the tree of life could survive even if a lot of its branches were lopped. Some arcane reasoning and mathematics is involved and Professor May is perfectly capable of defending his position for himself. I prefer to take an economist's line: it is not biodiversity that matters, in the sense of the maximum variety on Earth. What matters is something rather different, which I will call 'revealed biodiversity'. The 18th-century Irish Bishop, George Berkeley, laid down this line. Shorn of the caveats with which any philosopher surrounds his every argument, Berkeley's position was that existence consists of what is perceived. In its snappiest version, the tree in the college quadrangle does not exist when we are not there to see it.

By extension, as an academic might say, the wildlife of remote places is in effect simply not there if I cannot afford to go and see it. Maximum biodiversity is not what matters. That makes little difference to me; what matters is 'revealed biodiversity', the parts of nature I can afford to consume. The opportunity to enjoy the natural spectacles that remain in the world is what is of concern to me, not what someone mounting an expedition into the jungle may hope to find. A brutal way of thinking, of course, but then economists are very blunt individuals – they have never taken Keynes's advice to strive at becoming humble technicians, like their dentists.

Revealed diversity on the rise

Revealed diversity is on the rise. In the developed world, opportunities to consume nature have been expanding by leaps and bounds. All the equipment needed by naturalists is within reach. Binoculars, telescopes, cameras, field guides, information via the Internet, the real prices continue to fall rapidly. Cheap air travel enables respectable numbers of people to visit distant places to watch wildlife. The increasing migration of humpback whales up the east coast can be watched and so can all sorts of other biological events. People take four-wheeled drives and go around Australia to witness them. They go to Kakadu, they go to the Barrier Reef. I have friends who travel the Earth 'twitching' birds, building up the longest species lists they can, competing with others who have the same interest. You may dismiss them as rich people, and by the standards of their forebears and of most of the world's population they usually are, though this is seldom true of the students among them and the remainder are choosing to consume experiences of nature rather than big houses or flashy cars.

Instead of shrinking away, biodiversity in any meaningful sense is increasing. What is on the up is revealed biodiversity: the part of the natural world that can be commanded by real people. They can see the tree in the quad and whatever they cannot see scarcely concerns them. No-one ultimately believes, of course, that ecosystems which are out of sight do not really exist; even Bishop Berkeley did not go that far. Nor would many people, if pressed, admit that they do not care about genuine losses of wildlife elsewhere in the world. Adopting the Bishop's approach is merely a device to dramatise the issues.

The situation is surely not as bleak as conservationists make out. Eric Rolls, to my mind Australia's greatest environmental historian, used to say that there are now more trees in the country than were here when Captain Cook fronted up. No-one to whom I have repeated this has ever believed it but, given his first-hand ecological understanding, my money is on Rolls. Some of the supposed loss is political; it is just scare tactics on the part of the NGOs and individuals who make a good thing out of agitating their audiences and their subscribers with one new threat after another. Yet another part of the sense of loss is artificial, produced by selective reporting, which is easy because ecology is immensely complicated and constantly interacting in unforeseen ways. How the effect is achieved is by playing down the positive changes. Nevertheless, although populations may shrink, they may also recover. Some birds and animals have been introduced and others have invaded or spread; farming has been influential in creating new habitats. But the sleight of hand is to denigrate or ignore the newcomers. They are invariably considered to threaten 'native' wildlife. This takes a very static view of ecology or relies on historically short periods of observation.

Economics offers an analogy. Experimental economics shows that people regret losses more than they relish gains, and so it is with ecology. Retreating species are lamented, even though their numbers may be overflowing in other countries, whereas arrivals are looked on with hostility – until time passes and new generations of people come to value them as part of the living entourage with which they have grown up. All this is subjective rather than scientific. In reality, great interest is to be found in the birds of the backyard and weeds of the doorstep, as they battle to settle down in unstable environments. There are as many scientific puzzles and opportunities close to home as there are in the distant cloud forests for which naturalists yearn. But the stamp-collecting or list-making habit in many of us makes it hard to see things this dispassionately.

Nature comes back however much we try to expel it. Many of the environments created by humanity for its own ends are highly liveable for man and beast. Urban areas provide innumerable niches for plants and animals to occupy. At first sight cities may look forbidding to wildlife but they are nothing of the sort, witness the classic volumes on the natural history of London by Richard Fitter and New York by John Kieran. To take an example nearer home, does anyone suppose that the botanic garden in Melbourne is not a great nature-friendly environment constructed by humans?

The Crete scenario

'Ordinary' people are quite content with the diversity of nature available to them, even in the cities. Their attitude has come to be called the 'Crete Scenario', after the pauperised ecology of that island. Most people are scarcely concerned that the range of species around them is not super-large (though, counting invertebrates, the total is actually huge). They have pets, their children go on school trips to zoos, and they have the feeling that an enormous expanse of outback exists to which they could travel should they feel the urge. They place an 'option value' on the outback. They are not going to flog around Australia in Land Rovers, but they like to believe they always could and that, if they did, a mass of nature would be revealed to them.

The environmentalist, the academic, the eager naturalist and the intellectual snob will not find this satisfactory. Ordinary people, on this showing, do not know what is good for them and are reluctant to become disturbed about the loss of biodiversity, just as they have disgracefully resisted the bleating of their betters about global warming. But such a view of one's fellow citizens is extraordinarily undemocratic. More opportunities for enjoying nature are potentially open to them than were ever offered to their ancestors, who were too busy toiling to take a great deal of notice. The tax-paying citizenry today are those who are paying for conservation; who are the elite to tell them what their preferences should be? They show very good sense over what they like. Biodiversity does not greatly matter to the public. People intuitively understand that what matters is revealed biodiversity. And more of that is around than there ever was.

11

Foreign Investment Matters to Australian Workers

Asher Judah

For more than two centuries, foreign investment has mattered to Australia.

As a continental nation of vast natural resources, achieving our full potential has always been capital intensive. Due to our physical isolation, modest savings rate, small population and disparate economy, we have always relied upon foreigners to make our development dreams a reality.

Before European settlement, it was the Indonesians who provided indigenous communities with tools and pottery in exchange for aquaculture products. Between European settlement and the end of WWI, the British helped fuel the nation's public and private development. Through the provision of imperial investment and loans, the British supported the nation's early agricultural, mining, housing, infrastructure and colonial expansion. After WWII, the Americans became involved, using their global corporate reach and advanced technology to help build the national economy and boost the productivity of our manufacturing and resource sectors. Decades later, the Japanese did the same, but this time for real estate, tourism, iron ore and coal. Since then, it has been the Singaporeans, Chinese, Indians and Europeans who have helped meet the needs of an increasingly hungry global economy. Whether as nomads or settlers, farmers or industrialists, or technologists or tour operators, Australians have constantly relied upon foreign capital to grow their economy and enhance their standard of living.

In exchange for a decent yield and improved security of supply,

71

foreign businesses and governments have always been eager to invest in Australia. To our ultimate benefit, this interest has helped create jobs, strengthen local businesses, stimulate the economy, fund infrastructure and lift productivity, efficiency and competition.

Australian workers benefit

The Australian worker has long been the beneficiary of foreign investment, with many of our largest employers being foreign-owned. Whether it is teenagers at McDonald's, their older siblings at HSBC, or their parents at Toyota, the careers of thousands have been touched by foreign investment. Although, in some quarters, foreign investors are viewed as parasites of the Australian economy, their involvement has actually been responsible for creating much prosperity and employment.

Australian businesses are also better off. Through the introduction of new technology, equipment modernisation, improved foreign market access, underwritten expansion costs, consolidation of less efficient and end-of-life businesses, and by helping enterprises maintain international competitiveness, foreign investment has helped propel Australian businesses to higher standards. It has also facilitated innumerable joint ventures and the creation of vibrant new industries such as information technology and car manufacturing. As a result, Australia's business sector has been made considerably stronger.

Indeed, the economy also grows faster as a result of foreign investment. With increased capital and debt at our disposal, a greater number of projects have been activated, making more of the financially impossible possible. There is no greater example of this than in the energy sector where critical development opportunities have been unlocked as a result of foreign investment. Whether it is the North-West Shelf, Bass Strait or the Bowen Basin, foreign investment has been the driving force behind the creation of thousands of new jobs, increased tax revenue and greater demand for locally produced goods and services. Put simply, these projects would not have been possible had their foreign source of funding been lacking.

Infrastructure development is another area where foreign investment has worked wonders for Australia. Faced with the combination of huge distances, underdeveloped industry and limited domestic capital, Australia's infrastructure base would never have developed as quickly without the presence of foreign investment. When Australia's economy was in its infancy, it was foreign investment that helped fund our early utilities, transport links, and telegraph networks. Over a century later, its focus has shifted to privately funding the Pilbara's rail lines, our cities' toll roads, and the maintenance of food bowls' supply chains. Whether looking at the past or the present, it is foreign investment that has made much of Australia's infrastructure base a reality.

Further, Australia's productivity, efficiency and competition levels are also much better. The influx of new management techniques, new products, GM crops, and high-tech machinery has all helped Australia lift its maximum potential. Importantly, when one company is infused with such reforms, its competitors are forced to be as well. Foreign investment not only makes foreign-owned businesses better, it also makes Australian ones better.

Yet despite these benefits, and a greater than 20-fold increase in foreign investment since federation, Australians have never been fully convinced of its virtues. According to a 2008 Lowy Institute poll, 90 per cent of Australians believe 'the government has a responsibility to ensure major Australian companies are kept in majority Australian control'. Four years later, another Lowy poll found that 81 per cent opposed 'the Australian government allowing foreign companies to buy Australian farmland to grow crops or farm livestock'. What these two polls show is that regardless of our Government's official position on foreign investment, and our willingness to invest almost $1.2 trillion dollars overseas each year, the public remains unconvinced of its domestic benefits.

Over the centuries, Australians' hesitant embrace of foreign investment has ranged from violent opposition (racial tension during the gold rushes) to wilful self-reliance (the White Australia policy and industry protection) to economic nationalism (the creation of the Foreign Investment Review Board) to its most recent incarnation, geographically selective economic populism (opposition to non-Western investment). This hostility is deeply rooted in the misconception that foreign investment represents a loss of sovereignty, rather than simply the transfer of private ownership under the law. Referred to by University of NSW Professor Wolfgang Kasper as 'capital xenophobia', foreign investment is seen by many as the vehicle by which they are losing control of their economic affairs. This is not the case. Whether a business is big or small, international or local, it has to comply with Australian federal and state laws. And, despite what many may speculate, Australians are the only ones who can write them.

To most people reading a newspaper today, it is easy to believe that Australia is selling all of its assets to Asia. The evidence clearly shows otherwise. According to the Australian Bureau of Statistics, in 2011, China and India each represented less than one per cent of total foreign investment in Australia. Even Japan, Australia's largest Asian investor, remains only a modest contributor. Responsible for just six per cent of total investment, Japan is an important, but sectional player, at best. For all of the past century, it was not Asia that invested heavily in Australia: it was the United States and the United Kingdom. As host to two of the world's leading financial centres (New York and London), they are responsible respectively for 13 and 11 times more foreign investment in Australia than China and India combined. Interestingly, despite the duration of their dominance and the scale of their investment, neither attracts much media attention. Not only does this expose the hypocrisy of foreign investment's critics, but it also says something about the depth of the Australian debate.

Another key area of concern relating to the threat of foreign investment has been the perception that if farmland continues to be sold to foreigners, Australia may lose the ability to feed itself. That if we are not careful, we could end up like 17th-century Ireland where the foreign landlords (the English) owned the land and the locals (the Irish) slowly starved upon it. While this nightmare scenario sounds absurd in modern times, the threat of this future continues to retain strong currency in communities where the facts are absent and ownership changes have caused angst.

According to the Australian Bureau of Statistics, 99 per cent of Australia's 135,600 agricultural businesses and 89 per cent of our agricultural land is held entirely by Australian interests. Of the 11 per cent that is not, almost half is held by companies in which Australians own 50 per cent or more of the stock. Put simply, the foreign farmland takeover threat is a myth. Foreign ownership of Australian farmland has hardly changed in 25 years.

Australia is also not in danger of starving either. In a good year, Australia exports enough food to feed approximately 60 million people, almost three times our population. The reason we are able to do so is because we enjoy one of the biggest arable land endowments in the world. Over 60 per cent of the land mass is capable of agricultural production and this is a key reason why Australia enjoys a $14 billion agricultural surplus each year. And Australia is not in danger of being swamped with foreign produce either. According to the National Farmers Federation, Australia grows enough food to meet 93 per cent of its domestic needs. The food security crisis is a furphy.

Fears about the loss of Australian companies to foreign interests are also misplaced. Though Australian companies are often portrayed as the victims of foreign takeovers, many foreign investments take place at the request of those companies themselves. Indeed, over the course of two centuries, thousands of Australian companies have been made stronger by the actions of foreign investors, rather than imperilled by their presence. In the past four years alone, Victoria's Timbercorp was resuscitated by Olam International, Queensland's Cubbie Group was rehabilitated by Shandong RuYi and Western Australia's Gindalbie

Metals had its expansion plans made a reality by AnSteel. Rather than being responsible for the end of these companies and their workforces, foreign investment has in fact been their saviours.

Australian companies falling into foreign hands is also regularly misinterpreted as a threat to the economy. It is not. First of all, all formerly owned Australia companies which were acquired through foreign investment still make a contribution. Whether it's AWB in agriculture, Rio Tinto in mining or General Motors (Holden) in manufacturing, each company still pays Australian taxes, invests in the Australian economy, employs and trains Australian workers and consumes Australian products and services. While the ownership change may have resulted in profits going overseas, there is always more to a company than its shareholder returns. Second, it is often assumed that once a foreign sale has transpired, the process itself represents a net loss to the economy. In fact, the sale is the opposite. Once the funds change hands, the former owners have the option of reinvesting the proceeds back into the economy via the creation of new domestic assets or through the consumption of domestically products and services: something which occurs regularly. Rather than becoming weaker because of foreign sales, the economy is in fact made stronger.

Australia's foreign investment regime works

Of course, foreign investment is not an end in itself. If permitted to circulate unchecked, it has the capacity to undermine the national interest. Yet, to date, there is little evidence to suggest that this has occurred or will occur. Under the watchful eye of the Foreign Investment Review Board (FIRB) and its regulatory predecessors, Australia's strategic interests have long been aggressively protected. According to the OECD, Australia retains the seventh most restrictive foreign investment regime in the advanced world. Rather than being a soft touch, Australia is viewed internationally as having too firm a hand. Regardless of the international verdict, the domestic reality is there for all to see. Jobs are abundant, food is plentiful, ownership is diverse, business is competitive, the share market is buoyant and the legislature independent. Put simply, our foreign investment regime works. Despite constant warnings about the end of Australian sovereignty, Australia's destiny very much remains its own.

As a nation which relies on foreign investment to maintain prosperity, it is vital to remember that the world does not owe Australia a living. While Australia will always be dependent upon foreign capital, foreign investors will never be dependent upon Australia. Consequently, our ability to succeed over the long term depends upon our capacity to continually attract investment. In an era where capital transfers have never been more fluid or competitive, it is important that we get this aspiration right. To do otherwise would be to place Australia's future at risk. And for a nation with so much promise ahead of it, nothing should matter more than that.

12

Bittersweet Charity

Miranda Kiraly

It seems that charities need no longer be charitable. In 2010, the High Court handed down a judgment in the case of *Aid/Watch Inc v Federal Commissioner of Taxation* relating to the tax exemption status of charitable institutions in Australia. The case radically redefined the accepted definition of charity by holding that charitable organisations need not have the objective of relieving poverty by delivering financial aid. Instead, the Court held that the mere generation of public policy debate by an organisation regarding the manner in which governments tackle issues of poverty was sufficient to be a charitable purpose. The *Aid/ Watch* case rejected the long-standing common law rule that charitable institutions may not engage in political activity that aims to alter the law or government policy. This is known as the 'political purposes doctrine', and it has operated as a parameter to maintaining a legitimate and accountable body politic of charity law.

The broader consequences of this decision have cemented the rights of many small, politicised NGOs to be endorsed as tax-exempt charitable institutions despite not delivering any financial or non-financial contribution to the relief of poverty. This was the basis of the High Court's flawed finding in relation to the work of the foreign aid lobby group, Aid/Watch, who profess 'solidarity not charity'.

Unsurprisingly, the High Court's ruling was heralded as a victory by some in the not-for-profit sector, including Greenpeace and the Wilderness Society. To others, the *Aid/Watch* decision defied common sense for charity law. It came as the product of one of the most judicially activist High Court judgments in a long line of so-called implied rights cases.

The majority of the High Court saw fit to override the law and create an outcome more aligned to its own moral code by extending the implied constitutional freedom of political communication to charitable institutions. This was a far cry from its intended purpose of electoral participation. As a result, the High Court not only circumvented the long-standing political purposes doctrine of charities, but also constitutionally entrenched the so-called charitable sector's right to freely and legitimately engage in political activity.

The outcome cannot be easily remedied by a common-sense approach of successive governments. The fact that the High Court's ruling is based on solid constitutional grounds severely restricts the Parliament's ability to override the decision with legislation. Any legislative changes may pose a threat to the implied freedom of political communication.

Aid/Watch GetsUp!

The final and lasting effects of the *Aid/Watch* decision effectively allow the work of political advocacy organisations such as GetUp! and the Australian Youth Climate Coalition to also be potentially endorsed as publicly subsidised charities. In response to the *Aid/Watch* decision, GetUp! spokesperson Sam McLean remarked that the organisation would 'carefully consider whether to apply' for charitable status. As a result of the 2010 *Aid/Watch* ruling, GetUp! may well get up.

The 2010 High Court decision involved the charitable status of Aid/Watch. Aid/Watch is a small, grassroots advocacy NGO concerned with addressing issues of poverty and injustice through monitoring the allocation of foreign aid by governments. While it does not distribute any funds personally, its purpose is to lobby and engage public debate on issues surrounding the relief of poverty based on 'mutual solidarity, and on social and environmental justice'.

Aid/Watch makes no secret of its political motives. In recent years it has organised and funded various campaigns, which included sending an ironic birthday cake to the World Bank to call for its retirement, encouraging members to contact the Federal Government to pressure the Burmese military regime, campaigning against mining in underdeveloped countries, and actively petitioning against the perceived harmful impact of the Australia–United States Free Trade Agreement. As a result, it came as no surprise when it was unendorsed as a charity by the Australian Taxation Office (ATO) in 2006. The primary reason for the revocation was simply that Aid/Watch did not actually deliver any form of aid – it merely monitored the provision of foreign aid by governments and lobbied on issues where it saw fit.

The Federal Commissioner of Taxation had also alleged that Aid/Watch's lobbying activities breached ATO tax policy that 'advocating a political party or cause, attempting to change the law or government policy or propagating or promoting a particular point of view' will render an organisation liable to lose its charitable status. This was a policy that mirrored the common law political purposes doctrine and acted as a barrier to permitting lobby groups to advocate on taxpayers' dollars.

From 2006 to 2010, the decision faced several levels of appeal in a back-and-forth match between the ATO and Aid/Watch before reaching the High Court. At first instance, Aid/Watch successfully appealed the original decision on its merits to the Administrative Appeals Tribunal (AAT). AAT President Downes held that extreme political conduct might constitute grounds for an organisation to lose its charitable status; however, he did not believe this was evinced by Aid/Watch on the facts. The determination was made on the basis that Aid/Watch had a purported objective of relieving poverty – regardless of its methods for fulfilling these goals. The decision was later set aside on appeal to the Full Federal Court who dismissed the AAT's proportionality assessment, and found that it was bound by the political purposes doctrine, which disqualified Aid/Watch from charitable status. In making its determination, the Full

Federal Court also acknowledged the constraints of its role, deciding that such political decisions should ultimately be left to governments and not the courts.

The majority of the High Court mapped out an entirely different path in finding for Aid/Watch. It accepted that Aid/Watch had a dominant political purpose, and also did not deliver financial or non-financial aid. However, this salient factor did not act as a hindrance to the High Court successfully endorsing Aid/Watch as a charity. The majority came to the conclusion that Aid/Watch had a charitable purpose because its generation of public debate and political agitation surrounding the best methods for the relief of poverty was of significant benefit to public welfare (the fourth *Pemsel* 'public benefit rule'). Second, in order to be able to characterise its advocacy work as 'in the public benefit', the majority had to further conclude that the application of the long-standing political purposes doctrine excluding charities from engaging in political advocacy was no longer relevant in Australia. But perhaps most surprisingly was its final conclusion that charities' new-found capacity to freely engage in lobbying was in fact, a constitutionally protected right.

A constitutionally protected right to lobby

The fundamental relationship between the first and second conclusions of the High Court stems from two English cases. The first case, *Pemsel*, establishes a broad common-law definition of charity; and the second, *Bowman*, operates as a constraint to the application of the rule.

The modern definition of charity is found in the 1891 case of *Pemsel*:

> Charity in its legal sense comprises of four principal divisions: trusts for the relief of poverty; trusts for the advancement of education; trusts for the advancement of religion; and trusts for other purposes beneficial to the community, not falling under any of the preceding heads.

The fourth *Pemsel* head, 'purposes beneficial to the community' was used as the basis for the High Court's decision in *Aid/Watch*. The rule places a wide scope of discretion on courts to make a value judgment as to a perceived public benefit of an organisation and was thus curtailed by the 1917 case of *Bowman*, which set the framework and rationale for the political purposes doctrine:

> A trust for the attainment of political objects has always been held invalid, not because it is illegal, for everyone is at liberty to advocate or promote by any lawful means a change in the law, but because the Court has no means of judging whether a proposed change in the law will or will not be for the public benefit, and therefore cannot say that a gift to secure the change is a charitable gift.

The important relationship between the two principles has helped to maintain a strict demarcation between the three branches of government – one that rightly leaves the policy discretion of charitable institutions to elected and accountable bodies, and not the courts. The rule further ensures that organisations seeking to advocate a political agenda will not fall under the charitable umbrella due to any perceived 'purposes beneficial to the community'. However, the *Aid/Watch* case artfully circumvented the application of the political purposes doctrine in Australia by finding that charities possess a countervailing constitutional right to political expression. The case became a matter of free speech – and succeeded.

The cunning move surprised many observers of constitutional law because the implied constitutional freedom of political communication used by the High Court has its roots firmly steeped in a recognition and protection of electoral participation via the ballot box. The scope was never contemplated nor intended to extend to the realm of charitable institutions.

The High Court's introduction of a free speech argument was misguided. The right of Aid/Watch and other organisations with a predominant political purpose to propagate their own agenda via any lawful means of petition was never in question. The issue at hand was whether or not taxpayers should subsidise these activities. It was never a matter of stifling political debate. It was a simple matter of public accountability. The majority of the High Court categorically overstepped its jurisdiction in finding for Aid/Watch and masked its blatant judicial activism under the guise of implied rights.

The High Court's *Aid/Watch* ruling permanently transforms the concept of charity in Australia. It ensures that green advocacy groups such as the Wilderness Society and Greenpeace may no longer have their charitable status called into disrepute for their political activities. But more broadly, the result means that tax-exempt charitable status may now be legitimately granted to a wealth of activist lobby groups on the basis of a perceived 'public benefit' to democracy.

Chance to restore common sense

Accountability and common sense may still be restored to charity law post-*Aid/Watch*. This can be achieved through direct legislative intervention to create a narrow statutory definition of charity that explicitly excludes the recognition of lobby groups. At present there is no statutory definition of charity in Australia, which accounts for the heavy reliance placed on the common law.

On 1 July 2012, the Federal Government established the Australian Charities and Not-for-profits Commission (ACNC) to replace the role of the Australian Securities and Investments Commission (ASIC) as the regulator of charitable institutions in Australia. One of the many challenges facing the current Federal Government will be to introduce a statutory definition of charity by 1 July 2013 as a point of reference for the ACNC and all other Commonwealth agencies.

ACNC Interim Commissioner Susan Pascoe has acknowledged the difficulties that governments will face in coming to a single statutory definition of charity that excludes political lobbying activities. However, she has publicly stated that the definition will likely be 'codification of the common law' and not a broad, all-encompassing definition. It will be interesting to see what exactly the statutory definition entails and whether or not the Federal Government chooses to affirm the High Court's decision in *Aid/Watch*.

Regardless of the approach taken by successive governments as to what constitutes a charity, the significant hurdle will be to create a definition that does not offend the High Court's implied constitutional freedom of political communication held in *Aid/Watch*. Legislation that seeks to restrict political activity from the charitable umbrella will more than likely be rendered invalid because it could threaten the implied freedom.

The *Aid/Watch* case is not a win for democracy or free speech – rather, it undermines the fundamental freedoms it purports to uphold. The decision further demonstrates the dangers of judicial activism when the High Court seeks to descend into the realm of politics. Charitable status places a costly burden on taxpayers by showering a range of benefits – including income tax exemption, GST concessions, and a wealth of fringe benefits tax rebates for institutions. It is crucial that charitable status be reserved solely for organisations that deliver tangible contributions to the relief of poverty and hardship.

13

Family is the Fundamental Unit of Society

Richard Lyons

Oppressive regimes have sought to destroy the family

So often in the 20th century, mankind has been confronted with regimes that seek the elimination of the family as a primary and natural institution in the life of the people, and its replacement by the State as the primary actor in social life. The great atrocities of the 20th century totalitarian regimes were due in part by a desire to divorce parents from children, husbands from wives, and make all dependent on the State. Communist nations routinely took children from their parents to 'educate' them properly – and sever the natural link a child has with its parents. Part of Mao Tse-Tung's 'cultural revolution' was a systematic attempt to change the family unit from one of security, safety and love, to one where children 'inform' on their recalcitrant parents who disobey their Great God the State – all this in the name of 'equality' and the 'great leap forward'.

But there is something in this conception of the family – as an institution subservient to the whims of the State, as a product of mere convention, malleable to changing times or indeed, the need to create a more 'perfect society' – that causes humans to rebel. Families in communist countries fled. No-one was unmoved when they saw desperate parents attempting to cross the Berlin Wall, sometimes from West to East, purely because their children were on the other side. What those parents symbolise, in their attempt to reunite their disparate families, is a singular truth about human life: that the family is a natural

87

institution, not based on convention or the arbitrary will of the State but on nature. Every government that tries to destroy it and bring the family under its control ultimately fails, not from lack of trying, but because they are opposing an institution that can never be completely destroyed.

It is not just the more extreme ideologies of the 20th century that were at odds with some of the basic ideas of the family. Philosophies that often began with admirable motivations developed into social ideologies that often attacked the family and mischaracterised it. Feminism, which sought to pursue the admirable aim of removing discriminatory impediments to female participation in a range of cultural, social and legal fields (such as the vote, the right to work, hold legal and political office, etc.) developed in some quarters into ideologies that viewed the family as an impediment to women's progress rather than a vital foundation to it. Radical feminists characterised the family as a product of class conflict or gender 'socialisation'. For Christine Delphy and Diana Leonard the family was a structure whereby the exploitation of women became entrenched and existed for no other purpose but to serve the needs of the prevailing 'patriarchy'. It is no surprise that these radical conceptions of the family have not, in large part, caught on. The majority of women (as evidenced, for example, by the fact that the rate of divorce in Australia is in decline) do not view family as a device by which they are 'exploited' but as an institution vital to their own desires for children and partnership.

Theory of the family

The theory of the family as a natural institution is common throughout all human civilisations and cultures. The English political philosopher John Locke writes that 'The first society was between man and wife, which gave beginning to that between parents and children.' Here Locke echoes an extensive philosophical tradition on the origin of the family, one based on biology and natural relationships between those of the opposite sex. In explaining the origin of the family, Aristotle goes into more depth in his ethical treatise *Nicomachean Ethics*:

> Between man and wife friendship seems to exist by nature; for man is naturally inclined to form couples ... human beings live together not only for the sake of reproduction but also for the various purposes of life; from the start the functions are divided, and those of man and woman are different; so they help each other by throwing their peculiar gifts into the common stock. It is for these reasons that both utility and pleasure seem to be found in this kind of friendship... And children seem to be a bond of union (which is the reason why childless people part more easily); for children are a common good to both and what is common holds together. (Book VIII, Ch. 12)

In this passage Aristotle is attempting to explain why the bond of husband and wife is different to bonds of normal 'friendship'. The answer is simple, by nature Man forms couples, and those couples produce children, which, in turn, give rise to that institution known as the family. Aristotle, like a plethora of philosophers after him, notes that without the family, that institution from whence a natural bond of mother, father and children form, the political State is unstable.

Edmund Burke, the famous 18th-century critic of the French Revolution and one of the most respected English philosophers identifies this as one of the most important elements in a State. He writes that:

> No man ever was attached by a sense of pride, partiality, or real affection, to a description of square measurement. He never will glory in belonging to the Chequer No. 71, or to any other badge-ticket. We begin our public affections in our families. No cold relation is a zealous citizen. (*Reflections on the Revolution in France*)

If only more totalitarians read Edmund Burke! Burke, in responding to the 'Progressives' of his day, Thomas Hobbes and Jean-Jacques Rousseau, claims that the origin of the State is not in a 'state of nature' in which humans set up a state to avoid anarchy (in the case of Hobbes), or set up a state thereby destroying the idyllic life of a 'noble savage' (in the case of Rousseau), rather the State comes out of society and a country's culture, a natural outgrowth of human life, rather than an arbitrary creation. In his commentary on the source of government, the renaissance philosopher Francisco Suarez summarises this position, noting that 'Political power, however, did not make its appearance until many families began to congregate into one perfect community.' (*De Legibus*, Book. III, ch. II)

Beginning with the family and its 'affections' we establish more complex interactions with one another, forming a society with codes of conduct and institutions, which develops into political organisation and the establishment of far more sophisticated institutions and social relations, governed by 'governors' or rulers. It is this process of building; from family to society, to the State that Roger Scruton calls the 'invisible hand'.

The family, in forming such a vital basis for society has been seen by legislators throughout history as deserving special protection. From the very earliest societies marriage has been protected, as has the role children play in forming the next generation. Marriage has been seen as not merely as a 'private' good that affects only two people, but a 'public' good whose welfare affects the whole of society, not only the two adults who are a party to it. The reason why so many viewed marriage as a 'public good,' and thus a matter for legislation, is because it is the cradle in which the next generation is produced. It has a procreative purpose at its core and this procreative purpose is something we all need and all want to promote. Legislators from Ancient Greece to the modern day United States of America have heeded this call. Maggie Gallagher sums up this position with her slogan that:

> ... sex makes babies, society needs babies, and children need mothers and fathers. The critical public or 'civil' task of marriage is to regulate sexual relationships between men and women in order to reduce the likelihood that children (and their mothers, and

society) will face the burdens of fatherlessness, and increase the
likelihood that there will be a next generation that will be raised
by their mothers and fathers in one family, where both parents are
committed to each other and to their children.

The various courts of the United States have said something similar
to this view in a number of its cases on marriage and family. In *Maynard
v. Hill* in 1888 we find the court articulating clearly that marriage 'is the
foundation of the family and of society, without which there would be
neither civilisation nor progress'. In *De Burgh v. De Burgh* (1952) the court
outlines as part of its judgment the theory of the family that so many
philosophers have explained, that 'The family is the basic unit of our
society, the centre of the personal affections that ennoble and enrich
human life ... it establishes continuity from one generation to another;
it nurtures and develops the individual initiative that distinguishes a
free people. Since the family is the core of our society, the law seeks to
foster and preserve marriage.' *Conaway v. Deane*, as late as 2007, observed
that 'virtually every Supreme court case recognising as fundamental the
right to marry indicates as the basis for the conclusion the institution's
inextricable link to procreation.'

In Australia the Marriage Act since 2004 has made explicit what was
implicit in the original Marriage Act passed in 1961. It defines marriage
as 'the union of a man and a woman to the exclusion of all others,
voluntarily entered into for life.' Aristotle, Edmund Burke, John Locke
and other philosophers who originated the theories behind Western
institutions said nothing less. So, far from the totalitarian experiments
proving that the State should have nothing to do with marriage, they
instead prove the opposite. That it is good and healthy for the State to
encourage stable families and to aid children's development. It is true, the
State can often overstep its place and begin to impinge on civil society,
but it has a legitimate role in strengthening this public good.

In modern society some families are not necessarily the classic 'mum,
dad and children' configuration that is the norm, and while it is not for

us to pass judgement on families that are doing their best in imperfect situations, we still uphold the traditional, nuclear family as something to cherish. Our law acknowledges that it is not only traditional families that need our support, but it does – through its marriage laws and family laws – recognise the traditional family as deserving of promotion.

Not only does marriage serve such a vital public function, but social science research has also shown that there are health and well-being benefits that adults gain from being married. A recent book by Hon. Kevin Andrews MP documents many of these trends and studies. In *Maybe 'I do': Modern Marriage and the Pursuit of Happiness* Andrews explains how the *World Values Survey* undertaken between 1999 and 2007 shows the majority of adults still think marriage is important. The desire to get married has increased from 77 per cent in 1975 to 80 per cent in 1995. It appears also that surveys and research show that people that are married tend to be happy with their life and their marriage. In commenting on some recent social science research to this effect, the analyst Charles Murray contended that 'even without asking whether the marriage itself is happy, marriage is still a good bet for achieving happiness.' Andrews also delves deeply into the research outlining the benefits to children of growing up in stable families and the wider social benefits this can bring.

Policy retreat from families

Andrews argues that the conflict over the proper role of the family has been side-tracked since the 1990s, with the increased concern over the effect that a retreat from marriage is having on children. The million dollar question is, of course, what can a liberal state do to reverse this trend? We can consider a few basic principles. First, the family should be free to flourish and free from government intervention that makes its natural purpose difficult to fulfil (such as high taxes, punitive regulation and poor economic growth). Second, when the government *does* intervene, the regulation should support and encourage the family, rather than discourage it or try to take over its role. In this way, good regulation should always be *modest* intervention. Andrews outlines two principles that should underlie family policy:

1. Public policy should protect and foster marriage and healthy families
2. Wherever possible, public policy should support, encourage and utilise family and community organisations, rather than displacing them.

One of the most urgent areas for family reform is taxation, which often results in both parents being forced to work due to the high cost of living. Also important, writes Andrews, is counselling and education programs for married people. Most often this comes from churches and community groups and there is a possibility for the government to help sponsor these groups and ensure they remain intact at a community level. It would be ill-advised, though, for the government to attempt to eliminate the 'competitors' and make marriage and family counselling solely its domain.

In his speech 'The Forgotten People', the longest-serving Prime Minister of Australia, Robert Menzies, articulates where the life of a nation is to be found. Not in the 'great luxury hotels' or in the 'petty gossip' of the 'fashionable suburbs', or the 'officialdom of organised masses'; it is to be found in 'the home of people who are nameless and unadvertised', who see their children as 'their greatest contribution' as 'the home is the foundation of sanity and sobriety; it is the indispensable condition of continuity; its health determines the health of society as a whole'.

14

Why We Need Nation States

David Martin Jones

Great achievements

The state, sometimes misleadingly termed the nation state, is a good thing. This might seem obvious, but it is worth restating. It is a good thing for a number of reasons. The arrangement we know as the modern state emerged contingently in Western Europe from the confessional chaos caused by the spiritual claims of the Papacy, and the reformation's subsequent repudiation of those claims.

The modern state represented, therefore, a political solution both to this chaos and to the burgeoning jurisdictional mess that was the medieval realm. The doctrine of sovereignty that Thomas Hobbes discerned in the often-confused statecraft of the 17th century and promulgated in his masterpiece *The Leviathan* (1651) established the theoretical foundations for state authority. The sovereign state, in fact, made possible a coherent framework of political and economic order and provided the stable conditions necessary for the practice of the arts and sciences, as well as for exploration and innovation. Without it, as Hobbes observed, there was 'no place for industry, because the fruit thereof is uncertain and certainly no culture of the earth ... no commodious building; no knowledge of the face of the earth, no arts, no letters, no society' and we might add, no latte, and no Sass and Bide either.

The modern state made possible the constitutional protection of individual freedom and a market economy as forms of political and economic organisation. The institutions the modern state in its political

95

or democratic form has nurtured include parliaments, the rule of law, a free media and the provision of education and welfare. These are just a few of the more obvious goods the state and its bureaucracy have facilitated through, as Max Weber explained, its 'monopoly of violence within its territorial unit of rule'. More recently, the social psychologist Steven Pinker has demonstrated how the leviathan state was central to both the decline of violence and the rise of civilisation. In *The Better Angels of Our Nature* (2011), Pinker contends that '*The Leviathan*, a state and judiciary with a monopoly on the legitimate use of force, can defuse the temptation of exploitative attack, inhibit the impulse for revenge and circumvent the self serving biases that makes all parties believe they are on the side of the angels.' In Pinker's view, 'the centralisation of state power' led to a positive 'psychological change in the populace,' civilising the passions and creating habits of productive competition and cooperation.

From a somewhat different, sociological perspective, Ernest Gellner has shown how the structure of the modern state and its bureaucratic institutions formed the nation through a process of amnesia that forgot traditional, local and tribal attachments and replaced these with an homogenous culture and language. From this perspective, there is a big gap between traditional society and the modern state. In fact, it was the state that created modern nationalism or, more accurately, a uniform cultural identity in order to sustain and mobilise a population to economic growth and technological and industrial innovation. As Gellner explains, in his classic work on *Culture, Identity and Politics* (1988), modern society is 'literate, mobile, formally equal... with a shared, homogeneous, literacy-carried, and school inculcated culture. It could hardly be more sharply contrasted with a traditional society'. In this modern condition 'a man's culture, the idiom within which he was trained and within which he is effectively employable, is his most precious possession, his real entrance card to full citizenship and human dignity ... The limits of his culture are the limits of his employability, his world and his moral citizenship.'

In an increasingly interconnected but by no means integrated world, however, the modern citizen constantly bumps up against this limit and is acutely conscious of it. Thus culture 'which had once resembled the air men breathed, and of which they were seldom properly aware, becomes perceptible and significant.' Alien cultures threaten both integrity and identity. In other words, the modern state creates a modern cultural or national understanding which 'like prose becomes visible, and a source of pride and pleasure ... The age of nationalism is born.' Ultimately, the state created the modern world.

Threats and challenges

Despite these not inconsiderable achievements, new structural and ideological developments now threaten the coherence and identity of the modern state, particularly in its liberal democratic or open society form, and therefore its continued sustainability. Since the end of the Cold War these factors have combined to undermine both the idea and the practice of the modern state.

From a structural perspective, the globalisation of markets and industries has weakened the post-war consensus that served as the basis for the cohesion of the modern welfare state.

What Walter Russell Mead, in *Power, Terror, Peace and War, American Grand Strategy in an Age of Risk* (2005) terms the new, international, or 'millennial capital' driven by wide and deep, global financial markets has undermined state, or, regionally focused, capitalism. The Ford-era contract with the nation state that assumed that both worker and manager remained within a territory and even a locality no longer holds. This has upset the presumed harmonic convergence between capitalism and the social democratic state and has fundamentally transformed socio-economic relations. The new mobility cannot sustain a cradle-to-grave state-based welfare blanket. Instead, millennial capital, often depicted in terms of globalisation and deregulation, is actually about regulation to protect the existence and efficiency of markets, in order to allow wider access to their benefits. As Mead explains: 'national regulation may be decreasing, but the rise of millennial capitalism is creating new forms of international regulation that simply did not exist in the past.' Free trade agreements (notably bilateral rather than multilateral or regional) are much more than trade agreements: they create new transnational, forms of regulation and order.

The demographic changes that will redefine the social and political character of citizenship in the modern state, that is increasingly networked and slave to the behaviour of international markets that never sleep, also affect millennial capitalism. As population growth shrinks and goes into reverse in many of the developed democratic states, many of the socio-economic arrangements of the consensus and convergence era no longer make sense. We increasingly witness how welfare, health, education and pensions are inexorably privatised into market-driven, yield-sensitive investments, rather than treated as universal state entitlements.

The globalised division of labour and the death of the blue collar working class in the developed, cosmopolitan, global, capital city regions also has significant implications for liberal democratic practice. Policies that assume that only an elite-driven norm of multiculturalism can address the diversity of cultures in these modern global cities only increases the difficulty of sustaining state authenticated civil association in conditions of market fluidity, growing anxiety, and financial crisis. Bureaucratically engineered multiculturalism has not liberated, but, instead, imprisoned minorities. In the process it has transformed these culturally traditional minorities into an alienated resource for those who resent the modern Western state's secular liberal order. Such policies undermine rather than facilitate the modular or flexible behaviour of a citizenry necessary to sustain liberal democratic practice in an age of millennial capital and porous borders.

At the same time, from the internationalist and transformative ideological perspective that this structural change has facilitated, a *bien pensant* elite increasingly views the state as an anti-Progressive and otiose basis for political organisation. This new transnational class has formed from the media, academic and technology business, trade and finance elites. As Charles Murray has recently argued in *Coming Apart* (2012), this new class attends the same elite graduate schools, intermarries and assumes executive roles in government and the leading Fortune 500 companies. They have coalesced, over the last 20 years, to constitute an increasingly entrenched and interconnected transnational oligarchy which assumes that the nation state's assertion of its interests will inexorably evaporate to be superseded by regional or global governance and economic structures to deal with issues such as crime, trade or the environment.

In its Left, academic and multiculturalist version, more distributive, egalitarian and just forms of regional and global governance will replace otiose state regulation. Radical or cosmopolitan democrats, following Jurgen Habermas, consider that the state has passed its sell-by date and what needs to replace it is a form of global or cosmopolitan justice. International law and regional institutions already override domestic law and state sovereignty in many European states. Regions, from this radical anti-state perspective, constitute the building blocks for a transformational and emancipatory international order that ultimately envisages a form of global law and global democracy. In this understanding a democratically elected United Nations would serve as a template for a universal government enforcing global norms. In this context, the Hudson Institute's John Fonte identified, a 'transnational progressivism' that is post-democratic and assumes an internationally networked polity based on shared group consciousness rather than legal rights and global laws that transcend state jurisdictions. Its advanced guard takes the form of Non-Governmental Organisations (NGOs) that are unaccountable to an electorate and escape political checks and balances in order to establish global laws that overcome state constitutional jurisdictions.

The new order – EU

The quotidian governmental exemplification of the new form of order is, of course, the European Union. Somewhat ironically, Western European elites that gave birth to the modern state order are now deeply committed to the process of unravelling it. In the process they have created, at the heart of Europe, a post-modern, neo-medieval order of overlapping jurisdictions presided over by an unelected regional bureaucracy. The EU has, over a half century, centralised its authority and progressively eroded the formerly sovereign parliaments and national assemblies that emerged from the post-Reformation world to create the conditions for modern individualism, freedom and a secular order. The new Euro elite is not only democratically challenged, it is a political class that, for the first time in history, is both managerialist and radical pacifist in its orientation to order and control. This is evident both in its internal commitment to economic and welfare distribution between member states, and externally, manifested in its refusal to countenance force or a European military. Ironically, awarded a Nobel peace prize in 2012, the Nobel committee failed to observe that it was in fact the victory of allied states that brought peace to Europe after 1945. The European regional project, in other words, was a consequence rather than a cause of peace.

Over time, the EU's ideological commitment to political union at the expense of fiscal rectitude permitted, via the European currency union after 2000, the economically weaker states of Portugal, Ireland, Greece and Spain (PIGS) to use cheap money to fuel an asset boom. At the same time a lack of fiscal oversight allowed these weaker economies, of which Greece was the worst, to exceed their budget targets with impunity. The European Commission's ideological commitment to rolling back the state control of currency engineered a European financial crisis and the imposition of austerity on the weak PIGS as a price since 2009 for bailing out national debt. The political consequences of this post-democratic utopianism have not been a peaceful, just, cosmopolitan order, but an increasingly polarised and demagogic politics that facilitates not peace but riot and internal war, as the EU, despite its failings, continues to demand greater integration.

What Europe urgently needs, however, is a large dose of realism. This will entail a return to its master thinkers of the secular order – Hobbes and Machiavelli – rather than the utopian and anti-political managerialism that has worryingly distorted Western democratic thought and practice. Interestingly, and from a realist and sceptical perspective, it is pertinent that the states that have most successfully weathered the durable disorder of the twenty-first century are small and flexible and have not abandoned their sovereignty to pursue the chimera of regional and world justice. Thus, it is states such as Switzerland, Canada, Australia, Singapore and Norway who maintained their state institutions – rather than heeding the siren calls of transnational law and global redistribution – that will come through the current financial crisis intact and hopefully lead to a new respect in elite circles for the time-forged institutions of the nation state.

15

Intellectuals Do Not Matter

Greg Melleuish

One of the most distinctive features of our age is the presumption that intellectuals and the ideas they create are crucial for the health of our body politic and the progress of the nation. Thomas Sowell's *Intellectuals and Society* has a neat definition: 'an intellectual's work begins and ends with ideas.' Without their contribution apparently we would have to suffer being ruled by the ignorant and the ill-informed who normally go by the name of citizen, or even redneck or bogan. In the modern age, it is contended, the contribution of intellectuals is crucial if we are to create a prosperous and just society.

Of course, much of this argument derives from people who think of themselves as intellectuals. After all, as we produce more and more university graduates there has to be some sort of justification for such enormous public investment in universities.

Wedded to abstract ideas

The increase in the number of intellectuals in the modern age is a fact. That it has been a positive development is much more contentious. My argument is that the creation of a group of people wedded to abstract ideas has been as much a curse as a blessing as can be seen in all the murderous movements of the modern world from the Jacobins to the Islamists of our own time. Intellectuals, the disciples of 'mere theory', are to be distinguished from those who possess an appreciation of the proper application of the human mind to understand and better the world. Opposing intellectuals does not mean opposing the proper use of the human intellect.

I should like to begin by making three points.

The history of humanity is the story of the sometimes slow and laborious progress of the application of human intelligence to improve the way in which they do things. Human beings are very good at applying their intellect to solve practical problems, and one of the great beauties of the human intellect is that it is possible for people to devise ways of doing things in a better way. We would not have many of the complex things we have today if our ancestors had not made much simpler discoveries upon which we, as their descendants, could build. Human beings are naturally creatures who apply their intelligence to solve problems and overcome difficulties.

Ideas served up in an abstract and rationalist fashion, as models and mere theories, can be extremely harmful as their connection with the real world may be relatively slight. The history of the modern world demonstrates the harm which occurs when individuals or groups of individuals attempt to put their 'models' into practice.

Many so-called intellectuals are not necessarily gifted when it comes to matters of the mind. In fact, some of them can be intellectually mediocre and their ideas second-rate. But unlike sport where competition ensures that only the very best players rise to the top (leaving aside the freakish gold medal won by Steven Bradbury) the fact that someone holds a PhD or is a professor is no guarantee of the quality of his or her mind. Gaining a PhD is more a tribute to one's psychological stamina than one's intellectual capacity, while the capacity to network is easily the most important skill required by the aspiring professor. What passes for intellectual activity in Australia, especially on ABC1 shows such as *Q&A*, is often not of very high standard.

The English-speaking people have always felt uncomfortable with the term intellectual. This is because men and women of ideas have always had a more practical orientation towards their world and their ideas have accordingly been more oriented to practice as opposed to mere speculative theory. The English, like the Romans, but unlike the Greeks and the Germans, are not an especially philosophical people and this is reflected in Anglosphere countries such as Australia.

I am trying to make an important point. Human beings and the culture that they create is an expression of the human mind. We are, by nature, creatures who make constant use of our intellectual and creative faculties. It is, in many ways, our defining characteristic. There is, however, a huge difference between human beings making good use of their God-given intellectual capacities and a world dominated by intellectuals. In the ancient world a distinction was made between healthy forms of political order and degenerate ones. Hence an aristocracy, or rule by the best, had as its degenerate form oligarchy, or rule by a favoured few seeking their own self-interest. In a similar way we can argue that a world in which intellectuals matter is the degenerate form of one in which individuals make good and constant use of their intellectual faculties to solve problems and advance the common good.

People who use their intellect

So what is the problem with a world in which intellectuals, as opposed to people who use their intellect, predominate? It all comes down to the relationship between those who specialise in the matters of the mind and the wider society of which they are part. Such people, who we can call thinkers, have an important contribution to make to their world in a number of ways:

- Developing new and improved ways of doing things, especially in a practical way.
- Clarifying ideas and concepts so that we are able to think more clearly and deeply.
- Developing criticism of the existing ways of doing things.

- Taking ideas and seeing where they lead, including speculation
  on a whole range of matters that have no apparent practical
  import.

Thinking is an important human practice which should be encouraged for its own sake. There are forms of human intellectual activity, including solving mathematical problems, which are deeply satisfying and which relax the mind. Hence ancient thinkers, such as Plotinus, practised philosophy because it led them to a higher spiritual state.

The problem with intellectuals is that they tend to confuse the things of the mind with the realities of the world. They want to bend reality so that it conforms to their intellectual and spiritual longings rather than putting ideas and the world together so that a practical and useful outcome is achieved.

It is indeed admirable when individuals study ideas with a view to improving their capacities, or even in the hope of achieving a higher reality. The real problem comes when such thinkers, having escaped from the apparent darkness of their caves, then attempt to take the light they have discovered and impose it forcefully on others. They probably believe that they are bringing back the gift of fire, but in reality what they impose only scorches and burns.

It is this disconnect between ideas and reality that is at the centre of the problem of the intellectual. It is made infinitely worse by the mindset of the intellectual who believes that he or she has found the truth and must make it known. Anyone who spends much of their time in the realm of ideas knows that the greatest sin of the intellectual is that of pride. One becomes excessively proud of one's intellectual achievements and of one's capacity to make a better world. Such individuals come to believe that they hold the key which will unlock the door to that better place.

Francis Bacon commented that 'A little philosophy inclineth man's mind to atheism, but depth in philosophy bringeth men's minds about to religion.' The first flush of discovery puffs up the ego but prolonged study makes us humble because we come to appreciate just how little we know. The problem is that most intellectuals never get very far beyond 'a little philosophy' and glory in their possession of that littleness. The less they know, they more they believe that they can remake the world according to that knowledge.

The Australian social thinker Elton Mayo argued that an addiction to revolutionary creeds was a form of psychological disorder which was related to an individual's inability to interact properly with the wider society. He was horrified by the idea of teaching abstract social sciences to students, arguing that these abstract studies just further alienated students from their world when what they needed were the development of skills that encouraged social integration.

We do not have to follow Mayo down this road to appreciate that an excessive reliance on abstract thought has implications for how a person relates to the world. A diet composed only of abstractions is not a healthy one. Unfortunately, this is the diet of ideas on which the intellectual feeds. The situation is compounded by the contemporary obsession with intellectual 'models'. Once, people thought concretely, fusing ideas and reality. Today, ideas are turned into models that imitate the world without being the world. One has only to look at the debate on climate change to see the perverse consequences of relying on models rather than experience.

An addiction to abstract ideas is not good for the soul. It has been noted that when academics need psychological help they tend to deal with their problems in an academic way. They understand themselves in terms of intellectual models, not as real people.

The other danger of an excessive faith in abstract ideas comes from the despair that occurs when the world does not bend its knee and transform itself at the behest of the intellectual. Intellectuals thus become critics of their world. But their criticism is not founded on modesty and a desire to make incremental improvements that will benefit their fellow human beings. Rather, it proceeds from alienation, and from the disillusionment engendered when the intellectual discovers that those who have remained in (what he or she sees as) darkness will not change the world according to the 'you beaut' model that the intellectual offers. Those who have remained in 'darkness', prefer their common sense to the untested model of intellectuals. This leads, of course, to the denunciation of such common-sense folk as citizens.

Disillusioned intellectuals

Disillusioned intellectuals find not only that they cannot remake the world, but also that ordinary folk have little interest in what they have to say. Intellectuals retreat into their own world, seeking the company of the likeminded, and passing their time pouring scorn on the foolishness of the world for not listening to them. Their criticism becomes darker and more vehement and it is often an expression of their rage. The world has not given them the respect that they believe they deserve.

When they do come to exercise some influence on their world the consequences can be devastating. What we get is a mixture of intellectual pride and arrogance, combined with a hatred and contempt for what they see as the lesser mortals of the world, and topped with a deeply flawed understanding of how the world actually works. One has only to look at the influence of the climate change alarmist warriors to see just how bad the impact of intellectuals can be.

In a sense it is not entirely correct to say that intellectuals do not matter. Rather the problem is that they matter in exactly the same way that any social or political problem matters. Intellectuals cannot be simply consigned to camps in Marrickville or Fitzroy and loaded up with Arts grants and ARC grants in the hope that they will keep to themselves and not bother the rest of us. The problem is that intellectuals mostly want to change the world in ways that are deeply flawed.

The 'intellectual problem' of the modern world should alert us to the related problem of how we, as human beings, should make best use of the intellectual capacities with which we have been endowed. Of course we should make the best possible use of those capacities as we can but we should also be humble when we come to put ideas into practice so that we actually do good rather than harm. Brilliant ideas do not necessarily translate into brilliant practice. The world of practice is one that requires skill and measured judgement; it is place where one should have mastered an art rather than being expert in a purely theoretical science. It requires a style of human intellect that has not been seduced by abstract models. In such a place there is no place for intellectuals.

16

Financial Complacency in the Face of Three Economic Crises

Frank Milne

Conventional opinion about the international financial crisis that erupted in the summer of 2007 is that few professional economists saw it coming; nor did they anticipate its ferocity, which devastated the United States of America (USA) and European economies and financial systems and led to civil unrest and fears of greater violence in the European Union (EU).

Why were the authorities and public not warned before mid-2007? At the time, a tiny number of vocal 'cassandras' who delivered warnings in the media were roundly ridiculed. Now these prophets are lauded. What is not widely appreciated is that there were far more professionals who gave private warnings to the large financial institutions, government regulators and central banks. These people always tender their advice in private because professional analyses of dangerous economic risks are subtle, as well as potentially incendiary in the hands of political populists, irresponsible media pundits and corrupt vested interests. The last thing any prudent professional would wish is to precipitate a panic. It is a tragedy that many of those who gave private warnings were ignored, ridiculed or, in some cases, lost their jobs because they challenged the financial and economic conventional wisdom. It may have been conventional but it was far from wise.

Because the economic crisis is continuing and still imposing large costs on Western societies, it is crucial to listen again to the 'cassandras'. More importantly, there is not one, but three separate crises – international private debt, international productivity and income distribution, and Western fiscal policy. These three appear to be quite separate in origin and have been brewing for decades, but the economic stresses they impose have interacted, greatly magnifying their impact.

The consequences for the Australian economy could be severe. Although many in the Australian establishment have boasted that Australia is relatively immune, describing it as a 'Lucky Country' which has avoided the crises through wise policy, this is at best a partial truth. Professionals within and outside Australia have been warning for years that the country is not immune: downside risks have been increasing. Complacency is dangerous.

1. The international private debt crisis

The debt crisis first appeared in public in the USA housing market in mid-2007. It crossed the Atlantic and played havoc with international banks and other institutions that held the defaulting mortgages. Financially stressed institutions became only too aware that similar risky practices were common in other countries: Ireland, Portugal, Iceland, Spain and the UK.

Although the crisis burst into view only in mid-2007, its roots had been clear to shrewd risk management professionals by 2003. The international housing boom took flight, ultimately plateauing in 2006, and declining in the first half of 2007, but financial blogsites in the USA were ringing alarm bells much earlier and some astute bank regulators in the USA had battled to expose risky and crooked lending practices. Bank exposures to mortgage losses were obvious to professional risk managers, especially when probing questions were asked about the fragility of credit securitisation systems, credit insurance and counterparty risk.

Through 2007–2009, financial losses mounted and many large and small banks failed in the USA and the EU. Many governments panicked and were bullied, blackmailed or bribed into subsidising imprudent lending by large banks. Western political establishments prayed that these subsidies would buy time to sort out the mess that the complacent political, bureaucratic and financial establishments had created.

The roots of the Credit crisis are simple, although the details are subtle and complex. Bankers have not found new ways to lose money. The rapidly expanding securitisation of credit created perverse incentives for mortgage originators and securitisers to over-expand the construction of houses, consumer credit, car loans, and so on. Mortgage originators were rewarded for generating loan volume with little regard to default risk. Banks which packaged risky mortgages sold them to unsophisticated investors who realised too late where the risks were buried. The inevitable day of reckoning came when the absurd housing bubble burst. The USA and other governments had played a key role in providing tax and other incentives to induce poorer citizens to make capital gains on real estate. Alan Greenspan, chairman of the US Federal Reserve Board, Presidents Clinton, Bush and others in Washington peddled the story that real estate wealth gains were a money machine for the poor. This was a foolish fable: the end result has been to increase poverty – a classic example in public policy of the Law of Unintended Consequences.

Contrary to what is reported in the popular media, there were commercial banks, large and small, in the USA and elsewhere, that saw the mounting risks, and avoided most of the consequences. These banks had a strong culture of professional and effective risk management embedded in their organisations. Successful bankers require high intellect; serious mathematical and statistical skills; a deep appreciation of history and politics; and shrewdness in evaluating social and economic risks. Sadly, in far too many cases, not only did financial leadership fail, but also the governance, organisational structure and culture of major financial institutions were found to be wanting. Too many 'financial masters of the universe', who had mediocre banking and risk management skills – and wildly inflated egos – failed spectacularly. Some others, who survived either through good fortune or government bailouts, have deluded themselves that they are far cleverer than the evidence indicates. Thankfully, good bankers who understood the problems survived. They were prudent but are well aware that there are still substantial downside risks.

2. The international productivity and income distribution crisis

Since the mid-1980s, economists who study productivity growth and income distribution have puzzled over the decline in the growth of productivity and the stagnation of median male incomes in the US and other Western economies. Various explanations have been proposed: the increased participation of women in the work force leading to downward pressure on male incomes; increased use of computerisation reducing labour demand for manufacturing, clerical and other jobs; off-shore manufacturing, and so on. Recently, Robert Gordon of Northwestern University has proposed a more worrying cause. He argues that, historically, technical innovations have come in waves that created rapid increases in productivity before growth died away, leaving productivity at a higher plateau. The first great wave was the introduction of steam power in manufacturing and transport in the mid-to-late 19th century. The second began in the late nineteenth century and continued into the first half of the 20th century. It was a sequence of major innovations: electricity, telephone, radio, the internal combustion engine, aircraft, municipal water works and sanitation, and greatly improved medical techniques. This second wave's main impact had played out by the mid-1970s. The third wave was the computer revolution that began in the 1960s, but (according to Gordon) its major gains in productivity growth had been exhausted by the late 1990s.

Second, economists have been disturbed by a major increase in income and wealth inequality in the Western world. (The same phenomenon has been observed in China, India, Russia and other rapidly developing countries.) The media and politicians have seized on this topic, labelling it as the 1 per cent versus the 99 per cent. More detailed analysis suggests that increases in income inequality are due to increased profitability for innovators resulting from new technology; the explosion in the size of the finance industry; and more disturbingly the rise of corruption and rent-seeking as wealthy entrepreneurs lobby governments to reduce competition. The result is that new entrants have trouble eroding monopoly and oligopoly profits. This increase in rent-seeking has been accurately labelled as 'crony capitalism'. Assuming that there are policy measures to dismantle regulatory barriers to entry, remove implicit subsidies to large financial institutions, and increase competition, the incomes of bankers and monopolists should return to lower and more normal historical levels.

It is hard to predict whether slower productivity growth and more extreme income and wealth inequality is a passing phase. Innovations and the development of new ideas cannot be taken for granted. If innovation slows for a few decades, implying an extended period of slow growth in real incomes per capita, it will have serious consequences for pension planning, redistribution policies, and ultimately long-run budgetary policy.

3. The crisis in Western fiscal policy

The first two crises have important implications for fiscal policy. The decline in productivity growth had been apparent for many years and had been discussed by policy analysts, particularly those analysing the viability of pension and health care systems. Because the problem had been perceived as a long-run issue, the media and political establishment treated it either as an aberration or a problem for future governments and largely ignored it. By reducing taxation revenues and increasing expenditures on social and fiscal stimulus packages, the credit crisis and the resulting recession simply exacerbated underlying fiscal problems.

Far from being a new problem, demographic and other projections had for some time indicated that gradual reforms and adjustments were preferable to last-minute panic reactions to a long-run, slowly escalating problem.

Is Australia different?

Australia claims that it is different from other Western economies. In particular the official line is that it avoided the horrors of the credit crisis observed in the USA and EU through judicious fiscal policy and prudential financial regulation. The suggestion is that by exploiting Australia's (relative) proximity to Asia, the country's economy, powered by commodity exports to China, will continue to grow. Both arguments are highly dubious.

Australia has experienced a sequence of commodity cycles over its history. The current episode is running true to form. Given a sharp increase in international demand, commodity prices will rise above long-run marginal costs of production. This will lead to short-run excess profits and attract an expansion of supply from domestic and international suppliers. As international supply catches up with demand and/or demand falls, prices fall, imprudent suppliers fail, and lenders suffer losses. The downside risks are only too obvious to anyone who knows economic and financial history – and risk management. Observation of the commodity markets over 2012 shows that the downside risks have begun to materialise. The 'going to infinity with China' fantasy is looking increasingly foolish.

Australia benefited greatly from the Chinese government's fiscal expansion in 2008. During 2007 and 2008, China suffered a major fall in manufactured exports to the West. China responded with a massive infrastructure-building program that sharply increased demand for iron ore, coal and other commodities. Australia, Canada, Brazil and other commodity exporters were beneficiaries. Shrewd international observers queried the longevity of this boom. Due to internal stresses, China is attempting to change the direction of its economy and reduce infrastructure construction. Expanded capacity on the part of international commodity suppliers is also depressing prices. Both factors increase downside risks for Australian commodity export revenues. To add to producer woes, government regulations and taxes are increasing the costs of production.

The Australian Government panicked in October 2008, with a poorly planned and executed fiscal expansion. This increase in domestic demand was compounded by a sharp expansion in the mining industry. The resulting boom created distortions and dangerous future downside risks. The mining industry risks are now obvious. But international observers have long been critical of the country's real estate bubble, the dangers of high private debt levels, credit exposures, and the scale of foreign borrowing by the domestic banking system. Australian officials have dismissed these concerns. But recently official nervousness has become evident and the risks have become more obvious to the complacent Australian establishment.

Basic economic logic and market forces that operate overseas are not suspended at the country's immigration barriers. Nationalists and fantasists would like Australia to be 'different'; a 'Lucky Country' where economic water flows uphill. But sooner or later, these forces will retaliate with painful consequences. Keith Hancock remarked in his *Australia* (1930) '... the crisis, when it comes, is likely to be prolonged and severe. The wretched Government has so many scraggy chickens, and when they come home to roost they will seem to come at the same time.'

17

Does Respect Matter?

Kerryn Pholi

We understand 'respect' as a feeling of positive regard for another; of recognising, valuing, admiring, appreciating and honouring them. While we often debate whether the sentiment of respect is a universal entitlement or if such respect must be earned, we take it as a given that this sort of respect *matters*, and that people, especially marginalised and vulnerable people, suffer when they are deprived of it. Terms such as 'marginalised' and 'socially excluded' suggest that, for some people, their biggest problem is not poverty, ignorance or misfortune, but the failure of others to recognise and regard them adequately. We believe ourselves to be morally obliged to feel respect for others, and agree that respect is essential to a harmonious and just society. 'Respect' will prevent violence against women, will stop us from bullying and harassing others and will go a long way towards resolving Aboriginal disadvantage. If our respect for another individual proves too hard to sustain at close quarters, we can at least project the sentiment toward the 'social group' to which that person belongs.

What is 'respect' and how do we do it?

Our personal understanding of what respect feels like and looks like, and what we believe is deserving of respect, is deeply rooted in our social and cultural background, our upbringing, our experiences and our values. One person may show their respect through deference, and thus may avoid expressing their true opinions to me or challenging mine; another may respect me by challenging my views as a social and intellectual equal.

One person may respect me by disregarding any differences between us, while another may respect me by acknowledging, recognising and 'celebrating' my differences. One person may respect me for my innate qualities and talents (*who I am*) while another may respect me for my actions and achievements (*what I do*). One person may be conditioned to respect me as a 'lady', while another may come to respect me *despite* my female status.

If I do not make my desires and expectations of respect clear to others, the form of respect they offer me, even if given in good faith, may fail to please me. My efforts to educate and coach another person to respect me in accordance with my understanding of the concept could be a rich and rewarding experience for both of us, or it could very likely be a painful and ultimately exhausting process. If the form of respect I ultimately receive is largely the result of the training and prompting I provided, how authentic and satisfying will this outcome be for either of us? Would it be worth all my efforts, or would I have been better off simply accepting the other person's nature, accepting whatever they may feel towards me – respectful or otherwise – and devoting my energies to pursuing my own happiness instead?

In the arena of modern-day identity politics, 'respect' is vaguely described yet obsessively pursued as essential to the wellbeing and advancement of someone like me – a woman and a person of Aboriginal descent. It is, apparently, especially important that those who enjoy 'white privilege' and 'patriarchal privilege' appreciate and cultivate feelings of respect for my female and Indigenous qualities. I cannot recall experiencing or expressing a desire to be respected for these qualities; I would prefer that the 'privileged' simply respect my basic human rights and leave me alone as much as possible. Yet according to the logic of identity politics, receiving recognition and positive regard from people more powerful and important than me is what will deliver me from my present 'marginalised' status.

The apparent necessity of special forms of 'respect' for members of specific identity groups, combined with a lack of clarity around what it is meant to look like and a tendency to shame and condemn anyone naive enough to ask, has created a demand for expert guidance on these matters. Fortunately, there already appears to be a ready supply of experts to provide guidance on delivering respect to Aboriginal people, with organisations such as Reconciliation Australia and the National Congress of Australia's First Peoples largely devoted to this task. Should a current proposal (Human Rights and Anti-discrimination Bill 2012) to prohibit 'offense' and 'insult' to a broad range of identity groups become law, the demand for expert guidance on the respect requirements of a broad range of people with 'protected attributes' could grow dramatically.

We cannot know how another individual feels – whether 'respectful' or otherwise – unless we genuinely attempt to communicate with and understand them. Yet this does not stop us from confidently making assertions about the heart and mind of another; this one is 'a misogynist', that one 'a racist', the other 'a homophobe'. Our expert guides give us the language we need to identify and assign the most fitting label to an offender. The fear and shame surrounding these labels, and the stifling protocols and prohibitions that are built on this fear, erect barriers to genuine communication between us about our differences. Our aversion to, and repression of expressions of, 'disrespect' prevent us from openly examining what 'respect' could mean. Wherever powerful cultural taboos combine with vague and confusing rules to create a climate of fear, shame and suspicion, a host of experts inevitably appear to shepherd us toward righteous behaviour, and they usually profit handsomely in the process.

Respect is good – therefore disrespect is bad

The notion of the sentiment of 'respect' as a force for good reflects the narcissism of our age: *my feelings are vitally important to other people*. It is based on both a conceit that our personal opinion has a magically transformative power to enhance or diminish the dignity and wellbeing of another, and the assumption that other people – particularly those we regard as less fortunate than ourselves – need and crave our esteem.

In Australia, we are currently debating the extent to which the state can and should prohibit the expression of disrespectful opinions. James Spigelman, a former Chief Justice of the Supreme Court of NSW and the current ABC chairperson, recently demonstrated the squeamishness that some advocates of free speech feel towards its most extreme and confronting expression: so-called 'hate speech'. In his attempt to draw a distinction between permissible forms of disrespectful speech that merely 'offend', and unacceptable speech that 'humiliates, denigrates, intimidates' or 'incites hatred or contempt', Spigelman refers to Professor Jeremy Waldron, author of *The Harm in Hate Speech*, to explain why 'hate speech' requires special attention:

> Laws restricting hate speech should aim to protect people's dignity against assault ... Dignity in that sense may need protection against attack, particularly against group-directed attacks ... It understands dignity as a status sustained by law in society in the form of a public good.
>
> [T]o protect people from offence or from being offended is to protect them from a certain sort of effect on their feelings. And that is different from protecting their dignity and the assurance of their decent treatment in society.

Spigelman and Waldron's stance on hate speech is based on the presumption that my personal dignity, or that of my 'group', is contingent upon the opinion of others, and I therefore require special protection from publicly denigrating attacks that may negatively influence the way that other people regard me, or regard my 'group'. Would Spigelman and Waldron see their dignity, or the dignity of their social 'group' as being so fragile? I doubt it. Such well-intentioned arrogance insults my dignity in a way that another's malicious remark could never do.

The opinions that others may choose to express, including opinions based in hatred and bigotry, have absolutely no bearing on my dignity. My dignity resides within me; it does not require legal protection from 'assault', as no assault can shift it. If I am the subject of hate speech, my dignity remains intact; if anything, it is the speaker's dignity that is compromised by their own discourteous behaviour. If my feelings are hurt by the words of another, I may retaliate with words of my own or find other ways to deal with my feelings; I have no business demanding that my feelings should not be hurt. If my reputation is slandered, I can seek redress through the law. If I am exposed to public ridicule I may be embarrassed or humiliated (particularly if there was truth in the exposure and some justification in the ridicule), but my dignity is not lost unless I respond in an undignified manner. Spigelman and Waldron may be far more accomplished and influential than I, yet they do not have the power to 'protect' my dignity, just as no-one else has the power to diminish it. My dignity can only be preserved or diminished by my own actions, not by the words or the actions of another.

Prohibition of 'hate speech' lends irrational ideas more substance than they deserve. When we move to gag an individual's expression of bigoted opinions, we act as though we believe their views to be dangerous – whereas permitting the free expression of bigotry shows we have nothing to fear. Nonsense persuasively expressed can be powerfully seductive, yet the more we respond to it rationally and dispassionately, without fear or outrage, the more we will temper its influence on softer heads. Such an approach will require self-discipline on the part of governments and others in gatekeeper roles, in the face of public pressure to use their power to 'stamp out' hatred and bigotry.

The government's proposal to repress speech that offends, insults, humiliates, intimidates or denigrates may be based in benevolent arrogance, or it may indicate a lack of self-discipline. Either way, this is what happens when we allow our fears and others' vested interests to obstruct honest conversations about how we should relate to each other. People in positions of authority feel anxiety in the wind, take it upon themselves to decide how we should speak and behave, and they frequently get it terribly wrong.

You either have good manners or you do not

Fortunately, my life and my wellbeing do not substantially depend on the fickle preferences of those around me. While I hope that others will respect the laws that protect my basic rights and freedoms, it matters little whether they particularly respect me as an individual, except when a particular person's respect is something I wish to attain. The vague, cloying sentiment we call 'respect' – the feeling we are told we ought to feel, or at least ought to *pretend* to feel towards each other – does not matter. It is impossible to govern one's own feelings towards another human being, let alone govern the feelings of a nation – despite ambitious governments' best efforts of propaganda, surveillance and foolish legislation.

'Respect' as a series of protocols, behavioural guidelines, acknowledgements and rituals does not matter. You either have good manners or you do not, and you either care about this or you do not – and others will judge you accordingly. Guidelines and protocols are useful for those who care about manners and wish to refine them, and rules for respectful behaviour are helpful for civilising small children. Yet when etiquette becomes law, we are no longer demonstrating respectful behaviour, we are merely delivering compliance. If we believe respectful behaviour is an important social good, we must give each other the freedom to practice respect – or not – authentically, without coercion.

If I have very little respect for another person, whether for reasons sound or baseless, it is – paradoxically – more respectful for me to be honest with that person about my opinion of them than to pretend otherwise. Those who demand respect from others as an entitlement may – again, paradoxically – gain more of the respect they seek when they cease to demand it and demonstrate their ability to function in its absence. Behaving like a grown-up is not always gratifying, and being treated as a grown-up is not always pleasant – but it is always preferable to the alternative.

18

Privatise the ABC

Tom Switzer

L et me stress from the outset that I think the ABC is a great and important Australian institution, and many of its staff members – from Chris Uhlmann and Melissa Clarke on ABC1 to Sandy Aloisi and Glen Bartholomew on News Radio – are highly professional and intelligent members of the 'fourth estate'. I rather like Mark Scott, the managing director, who has expanded ABC services to vastly more people than any time in the corporation's eight decades. I am also a regular contributor to its television and radio programs, and I am proud of my association with them.

Group-think prevails

But one can make these observations, and still believe that the ABC should be privatised. Why? Because a soft-Left 'group think' clouds its editorial content, which alienates large segments of the Australian public. Group-think, together with expansion into the Internet and digital broadcasting makes the case for a taxpayer-funded broadcaster highly questionable.

Of course, the ABC is not calculatedly partisan, nor do its masters pull the strings in any marked way. But there is little doubt that an entrenched Left-liberal bias – or perhaps mindset is a better word – seriously undermines the ABC's claim to be an impartial provider of news and current affairs. If 'Aunty' were sold off, no-one would really have grounds for complaining that it is impossible to watch the ABC for a whole evening without once shouting at the television screen. After all, the broadcaster would no longer be bound by its charter to be even-handed.

In fairness, a lot of ABC news output is professionally produced and almost always on the pace. It is just that when an investigative documentary or current affairs segment – or a drama, comedy, entertainment or religious program – expresses an attitude or a tone of voice, it is a Progressive, Leftist one, albeit subtle and insidious.

What Boris Johnson has said of BBC journalists could be said of their brethren in the Antipodes. 'All their instinct and culture is to support state funding over the private sector – which is not surprising, since they are state-funded themselves.' He further asserts, 'In any argument they will instinctively gravitate to what they think is the most civilised and liberal option, irrespective of the merits of the case.' In the Australian context, they are located on a political spectrum running from Malcolm Turnbull, via Andrew Wilkie towards Tanya Plibersek and Christine Milne.

On every issue of political controversy, the ABC's mental default position is essentially left-of-centre: opposition to labour-market deregulation, anti-terror laws and tough border protection; support for a republic, multiculturalism and same-sex marriage; an obsession with gender issues, Aboriginal rights and catastrophic man-made global warming; and a deep suspicion of Tony Abbott, neo-conservatives, economic rationalists, climate sceptics, the 'Christian Right'. These groups will not get the soft interview.

No wonder the ABC, as Gerard Henderson often observes, cannot point to a prominent conservative or non-Left screenwriter in its ranks. And no wonder ABC journalists tend to be completely caught out by episodes such as the public backlash against the carbon tax or widespread community support for offshore processing.

No program sets the terms of the debate better than *Q&A*. On topics such as refugees, gay marriage and climate change, its coverage is loaded. Its choice of guests is always unbalanced. Its host Tony Jones is incorrigibly biased. It employs double standards in treating conservatives far more roughly than the opposites. Much of its questioning rests on a series of highly Leftist ideological assumptions. All of this, moreover, is before a studio audience which treats anyone who strays from the Progressive consensus with shock and distaste.

Then there is *Insiders*. Although a Right-leaning commentator is accommodated (nearly) every Sunday morning, they are always outnumbered by two more left-liberal counterparts and more often than not host (and former Labor media adviser) Barrie Cassidy. The token conservative's input, moreover, is often regarded by the other panellists as an outrageous contribution to the debate.

All of this explains why certain stories that would appeal to more conservative consumers are played down. Take the example I have often cited: Ronald Reagan. During the week of the conservative lion's death in June 2004, *Lateline* ignored the Republican president's life and times. No stories, no features, no debate. Yet several months earlier, the presenter went weak at the knees remembering John F. Kennedy 40 years after the liberal lion's death. Instead of affording similar treatment to a conservative icon – much less having a debate about Reagan's place in history – *Lateline* paid tribute to another American legend who died that week, musician Ray Charles. For good measure, the presenter browbeat foreign minister Alexander Downer on Australia's (as it turns out) non-role in the Abu Ghraib scandal in Iraq.

Some might argue that since Mark Scott became managing director in 2006, the ABC's revamped news division covers all big breaking stories. How that explains ABC24's decision to screen documentaries about Belgian identity issues after the Japanese tsunami in 2011 is not clear. What is clear is Aunty's selective news judgement. Immediately after Gore Vidal's death in August 2012, *Lateline* ran a sympathetic 20-plus-minute segment on the radical writer, including a long, soft interview with Foreign Minister Bob Carr from the Middle East. Which prompts the question: did the (left-wing) literary identity deserve so much live coverage even though the same presenter and program failed to run a story on a (conservative) political giant?

A pattern of bias

All of this reflects a pattern. When Milton Friedman died in November 2006, the ABC media hardly covered the Nobel prize-winning free-market economist; yet the ABC dedicated a lot of air time to mark the passing of interventionist economist John Kenneth Galbraith a few months earlier. When anti-terror laws make the news, the ABC all too often interviews experts on this subject, usually civil libertarians; and, sure enough, they agree that the laws, supported by both government and opposition, are draconian.

On climate change, much to the chagrin of its former chairman Maurice Newman, the ABC has jettisoned all semblance of impartiality; it campaigns with a consistent stream of scare stories. Yet it devotes very little attention to climate-gate scandals, any scholarship that challenges the warming orthodoxy and the United Nations' consistent failure to reach a binding global deal to reduce emissions.

More honest friends of the ABC insist Aunty is needed to balance the so-called shock jocks on commercial radio and right-wing newspaper columnists. The argument goes, what difference does it make that ABC journalists are Lefties? But those who hate talk-back radio or Rupert Murdoch's tabloids can take solace in the fact that they are not financing Alan Jones or Andrew Bolt. Taxpayers who subsidise the ABC to the extent of $1 billion a year do not enjoy that peace of mind. Remember the need for balance and fairness is there in the ABC Charter: it is the legislative quid pro quo for public funding.

How then to fix the ABC's well-entrenched group think? The ABC could recognise that the corporation exists within a cultural bubble. That is precisely what several distinguished BBC journalists and managers have done in recent times. In 2006, at a seminar convened to discuss how best to safeguard impartiality, Andrew Marr – a leading light at the Beeb and no right-winger – conceded that the British public broadcaster 'is not impartial or neutral'. It has, he added, 'a liberal bias, not so much a party-political bias. It is better expressed as a cultural liberal bias'.

When anyone makes similar observations about the ABC, they are widely dismissed. But no matter how much the Australian public broadcaster swears blind there is no problem, the issue refuses to go away. Why? Because for many taxpayers, the ABC's skewed assumptions are most annoying.

Another way of addressing allegations of bias is to insist that journalists deliver news instead of opinion. Although Mark Scott is right to say that under his tenure the ABC has taken to finding different viewpoints with gusto, he is wrong to claim that ABC journalists carry 'no ideological badge and [push] no line'.

It is absurd to allow so many allegedly objective reporters and presenters a platform on *The Drum* (both online and television) or local radio to air their subjective judgments about controversial political views. It merely highlights the left-wing mindset. Who could forget Marieke Hardy who called for Christopher Pyne, a senior Liberal frontbencher, to be 'attacked by a large and libidinous dog'? Or Radio National breakfast host Fran Kelly who declared her support for the highly unpopular carbon tax. 'Bring on the certainty, I say, get the thing voted in'? Or economics reporter Stephen Long who advised listeners to 'man the soup kitchens and erect their tent cities' during the global financial crisis? Last year, Long called Scott Morrison, the tough-minded Coalition's immigration spokesman, a 'racist' for representing Cook, the scene of the Cronulla riots.

One could provide many more examples of ABC journalists revealing themselves as biased and compromising their editorial judgement, but you get the point. By allowing so-called objective hosts and reporters to give their (usually Leftist) opinion online or on air, the ABC proves itself fundamentally at odds with the thoughts and attitudes of the

Australian people, to whom the broadcaster purportedly answers. It also shows that it has essentially chosen to end its pretence of being a public service broadcaster. As a result, it has made the clearest case yet for its privatisation.

Let the market decide

If the ABC refuses to act like a rigorously independent national broadcaster, the need for political balance and all other forms of impartiality should end. Sell off at least the non-news service divisions and let the market decide. This is especially justified, given that the ABC uses tax dollars to create a market distortion by gaining an unfair advantage against commercial rivals, such as Crikey, Sky News, and book publishing.

In the media marketplace, as *The Australian's* Chris Kenny has argued, falling advertising revenue caused by a coincidence of digital evolution and cyclical forces is costing jobs and threatening the viability of newspapers and television stations. Why should a taxpayer-funded, free-to-the-consumer competitor be allowed to expand on their turf?

Friends of the ABC say that the public broadcaster provides a range of programs that would not be found elsewhere, or would be unaffordable otherwise. They also argue that many viewers and listeners feel at home with the public broadcaster and that its programs are appreciated by a large slice of the public (which happens to be an economically and intellectually up-scale audience).

But if the ABC has value not only for the prime television and radio spectrum it occupies but also its quality programs, why would the marketplace let this valuable franchise die? If it were a commercially viable entity, how would privatisation diminish the quality of its product? Selling off the ABC may eliminate much of the Leftist influence elsewhere, but that would merely mean the Jonathan Holmes and Phillip Adams and Julian Morrows of the ABC could take their chances in the private sector.

ABC defenders also believe that rural areas should have at least some access to ABC programs; and that privatisation will hurt regional Australia's links with the media. But although there was truth to this argument during much of the corporation's 80-year history, the broadcasting landscape has changed utterly in recent times. As Pete du Pont has argued in the *Wall Street Journal*, 'cable and satellite have provided a buffet of interesting news, cultural and educational offerings for years. And the Internet – with its ubiquitous availability in homes, schools, and libraries, and on cell phones, iPads and Kindles – provides far more information than public broadcasting ever could'. Du Pont was making this point in the context of fully privatising the US public broadcaster. The logic applies to the Australian state-run broadcaster.

Last year Tony Abbott said that 'There is still this left-of-centre ethos in the ABC and I hope that Mark Scott continues to address it.' But the ABC's institutional Leftism is incurable. Only privatisation can solve the problem.

When the ABC is sold off and capital is returned to the federal budgets, the journalists could put on all the ideologically-tainted content they like. Some programs may not sell, and others will continue to aggravate many Australians. But at least we will not be forced to pay for it.

19

Australia Should Become a Superpower

Cassandra Wilkinson

Think big

A couple of years ago, Bateman and Bergin of the Australian Strategic Policy Institute (ASPI) suggested that Australia could be an oceanic superpower, pointing out that Australia controls five per cent of the planet's oceans. Since then, Australia has been called an energy superpower thanks to the Gorgon gas deal; an aid superpower thanks to growing development expenditure; and, a future food superpower.

But nobody seems to discuss with any seriousness the potential for Australia to become an actual superpower. Already this century has been given away to Asia without talking about what Australia could do to secure its position. The idea of Australia becoming a superpower may seem laughable – it has a small population, a few territories and a limited military capability. As the ASPI's Mark Thomson has observed, Australia's security relies on free-riding the United States of America.

On the other hand, Australia is geographically the sixth largest country in the world, with massive energy resources and an almost unlimited supply of potential new citizens and good ideas. The so-called 'natural limits' on population in a 'dry continent' can be overcome by use of nuclear power, which could create more than enough low-carbon energy to desalinate or recycle water for irrigation and drinking. One only has to look to the flowers being exported from Israel to see what can be done to overcome presumed natural limits.

Australia has everything it needs to succeed, not as Asia's quarry

133

or even its food bowl, but as its most powerful neighbour. Lack of
ambition, not a lack of ingenuity or resources is the only limiting factor.
In his 1889 Tenterfield Oration, Sir Henry Parkes among many political
and cultural leaders believed Australia would, in fairly short order, take its
place among the leading nations of the world.

> In this country of Australia, with such ample space, with such in-
> viting varieties of soil and climate, with such vast stores in the
> hidden wealth under the soil, with such unrivalled richness on all
> hands, and with a people occupying that soil unequalled in all the
> whole range of the human race in nation-creating properties, what
> is there that should be impossible to those people?

Canberra was designed to give a built form to these grand ambitions.
Speeches at the time called for an Australian capital to rival Paris, Chicago
and London. Although these speeches no doubt elicited their share of
sneers, it is striking how few speeches are made today calling hearts and
minds to forge a nation the equal of any great power. There are few
leaders who would champion an Australian century. Politicians talk,
sometimes begrudgingly, about sustainable growth, including population
growth. None mentions growth in power or influence and certainly
not in military might. It is hard to find a politician who believes in 'big
Australia' let alone aspiring to a place at the high table.

Public debate over Australia joining the UN Security Council had
most commentators branding the exercise a waste of public money, that
the appointment was an act of unearned self-aggrandisement, somewhat
embarrassing for a country out of its league. While Labor leader Doc
Evatt saw the United Nations as an opportunity for Australia to be a
middle power influencing its 'great and powerful friends', some appear to
think that even middle power ranking is an ambition above our station.

Great and powerful friends

During the great wars, Australia looked first to the mother country
and then to a big sister, the USA. In the case of another big war, for

many years the policy assumption was that these friends would defend Australia. It was also assumed that as the most developed country in a relatively under-developed region, Australia would, with a few good planes and ships, remain impervious to local assault.

But the neighbourhood has changed greatly since the signing of the ANZUS pact. Although the USA is still the most powerful actor in the region, the growth of wealth and population in Asia means the USA is not what it was at the end of the war in the Pacific. Hugh White wrote last year in *The Monthly*, 'the era of Asian stability based on uncontested American primacy has come to an end ... We therefore face a much greater risk of major-power rivalry and conflict in Asia over the coming decades.'

The rapid economic development of the region means stronger military forces nearby, not all of them controlled by friendly democracies. Indonesia is a non-threatening neighbour. It has become stronger and richer and has been slowly becoming more democratic. But that journey is by no means either certain or complete. While invasion from the North is clearly unlikely, it is interesting to consider for a moment how the East Timor independence conflict might have played out under a less benign scenario.

Becoming a superpower is not merely an end in itself. The pursuit of power for its own sake is the dream of the tyrant rather than the nation builder. There are strong moral reasons to embrace what may seem at first a greedy dream of an Australian century. The greatest moral reason is the Australian 'way of life' – laws, social mores and commitment to a Westminster system of parliamentary democracy. This way of life has been expressed differently at different times, but in the vernacular it has always been summed up as belief in 'the fair go'. While there is no Bill of Rights, the fair go is the common understanding of the American Declaration of Independence, 'truths we hold to be self evident'.

Former Governor-General Sir Ninian Stephen once observed on returning from overseas that one could feel the Australian egalitarian spirit on descent at Tullamarine or Kingsford Smith airports. Despite the existence of some class and social demarcations, Australia has committed itself to equality in rights and dignity regardless of wealth or status.

The fair go requires a form of government in which the citizen is sovereign. The fair go requires at the very least equality before the law, a universal franchise and the freedom to pursue whichever goals an individual seeks. Only liberal democracy is compatible with the fair go. Sadly, most citizens around the world do not share the experience of the fair go. According to Freedom House, all but four countries (Burma, Vatican City, Brunei and Saudi Arabia) claim to be democratic. In truth around 60 per cent of the world's population live in non-democratic countries and many nations that are democratic are fledging, partial or compromised by traditional systems of gender and ethnic prejudice, religious discrimination, caste, clan or corruption. Their citizens are yet to experience the full benefits of democratic participation.

Wherever liberal democracy blooms in the world, enemies beset it. In the last decade, six countries were deemed by the Nobel organisation to have become more democratic (Togo, Bhutan, Maldives, Pakistan, Thailand and Montenegro) but eight became less democratic (Gabon, Lesotho, Mauretania, Senegal, Afghanistan, Kyrgyzstan, Bahrain and Jordan). In Venezuela and Russia, rulers have altered or dodged the constitution to extend their terms. The world is watching Egypt enact a theocratic constitution as the *Arab Spring* experiences a winter chill.

At the end of the Cold War it seemed democracy was the inevitable end point of political reform. It was said that the West had won. But as Russia backslides it is clear that the enemies of liberty did not accept 'the end of history'. It is equally clear that liberty cannot be bequeathed. Each generation must preserve their own liberty from assault and raise their children to be eternally vigilant. Some fledgling democracies are under threat from internal illiberal forces such as the Islamic extremists who nipped in the bud the flowering of Egyptian democracy. Once these autocrats gain power, the marvels of modern technology and globalisation mean that they have unprecedented opportunity to damage even thriving democracies.

The 2008 Defence White Paper notes many of the non-democratic countries are flouting international bans on acquiring ballistic missile systems, and developing weapons of mass destruction. Several governments have become state sponsors of terrorism and others are simply so incompetent that non-state actors have become powerful rulers of regions within nations capable of initiating conflict independently, as Hezbollah did by attacking Israel from Lebanon. In this context, defence of sovereign territory is not the greatest existential challenge. Although Australia is clearly safe in the short term from state actors, it may be at risk in the medium term from the usurpation of power by non-democratic rulers or from powerful non-state actors.

The military challenge in this scenario is to support democratic nations to defend themselves. Failure to contribute to international efforts may see weak states become vulnerable to takeover by illiberal elements, which, if they succeed, could later become direct threats. It is not the immediate ambitions of near neighbours but the medium-term fate of the democratic nations of the world that will determine our long-term security. As the White Paper notes, 'Australia cannot be secure in an insecure region or in an unstable global security environment where the rule of law is not maintained'.

The small investment Australia makes in its defence is based on the broad assumption that the ANZUS treaty will protect in the event of an invasion. This view is sufficiently widespread to prevent concern about the decline in spending but somehow not well enough understood to stop complaints that Australia is too supportive of the Americans. To speak openly of potential threats posed by illiberal states in the region is deemed offensive to trading partners – code for not speaking plainly within hearing distance of China. But there are many democracies in the region closer to China than is Australia with historical reasons to be nervous about kowtowing.

Our greatest challenge

Kevin Rudd once called climate change the greatest moral challenge of our time. He believed it constituted the greatest existential threat to human societies. The numbers suggest otherwise. The greatest existential threat to human societies is, was, and may always remain, armed human conflict. More than this, instigators often use violence to achieve power over their adversaries and their own people. The end of war in many cases brings not peace and prosperity but a permanent state of siege favoured by victorious autocrats.

The execution of political opponents can extend under these regimes to the execution of whole classes of dissidents. This may be the 'bourgeoisie' under Stalin or Pol Pot. It may be aimed at entire ethnic groups deemed unsympathetic to a regime as happened in Rwanda between Hutus and Tutsis, to the Jews under Hitler and to the Marsh Arabs of Iraq.

Those regimes that use violence not only to gain power but also to hold it are more likely to oversee the death of citizens through aggressive enforcement of political programs such as the forced redistribution of assets and land. Autocratic regimes are more likely to preside over mass deaths as a result of ongoing hostilities with neighbours such as happened with the Iran–Iraq war. The decimation of perceived opponent populations and 'undesirables' by forced labour in prison camps is another form of misery. Jailing poets and homosexuals in Cuba, harvesting prisoners' organs in China and jailing the punk band Pussy Riot in Russia attest to this.

Scholars such as Applebaum, Gallately and Watson have argued that 'democide' or mass killing by government is essentially a Leftist/communist phenomenon. Given the contribution of Stalin, the numbers support a strong correlation. It is, however, arguable that the tactic is common to all autocrats, some of whom are communists, others of whom are simply cobbling together any old excuse for power. Adolf

Hitler invoked Nietzsche, Jesus and traditional folklore to justify his genocidal obsessions.

A more useful demarcation is Karl Popper's description of societies as free and un-free. Leaving aside Left and Right, religious and secular, East and West, there are places where citizens are generally free to do as they please and places where they are not. Australian citizens are blessed to live in a place where they are free. To ensure our children share those blessings it is not enough to hope that the USA continues to value a presence in the Pacific. It is not enough to pray that China becomes democratic before it gets rich. It is not enough to hope that the Indian middle class will propagate liberalism faster than populist politicians can mobilise the desperate poor with appeals to nationalism.

It is not enough to leave our fate in the hands of others. Margaret Thatcher wrote in her *Downing Street Years* that the first duty of a free country is to stay free. The only way to secure prosperity, freedom and our children's inheritance is to shake off the colonial mindset and claim a place as a world leader, making our own luck in an unpredictable future.

20

Progressives: Philosophy without an Anchor

Tim Wilson

Political Progressives do not matter because their attitude to people and government is inconsistent with human nature. One of the strengths of classical liberal and conservative philosophical strains is that they accept people for who they are and their lot in life. This philosophy does not mean they always like, or blithely accept the way people are, but their objective is not to use the power of government to conduct experiments to change individuals or their circumstances.

Progressives take an entirely different view. As a political ideology Progressivism is not what its advocates like to present it as. Progressives argue that their political ideology is forward-looking, open-minded and embraces diversity. They also like the word 'Progress' to be associated with 'Progressivism'. The irony is that Progressivism is neither forward-looking, that is, seeking progress, nor is it sufficiently backward-looking to enable its advocates to take stock of the lessons of history. Progressivism is also not an open-minded political philosophy. It is a political philosophy promoting rigid political and social values and actively promotes a straightjacket society of sameness and predictability.

Since the late 19th century, progressives have been unhappy with the results of liberal democracy and have sought to use government to change it. The justifications for using government by progressives include numerous objectives ranging from social justice to equity and equality to health. The foundations of the modern Progressive movement can be found in late 19th and 20th century USA and Great Britain. In the

USA they were called Progressives. In Great Britain they were called Fabians. Their tactics and their objectives were broadly the same. Great Britain's Fabian society foresaw many of the problems of achieving radical change through revolution and decided to achieve their socialist goals through the incremental justification for expansion of the State. Fabians understood that radical change was likely to prompt opposition and preferred subtle change that would bring with it public support.

The common ground between these Progressive movements is the role of the State. In the USA Progressives were not socialist, but they adopted the same philosophy of using the arms of the State to try to regulate and legislate a more 'perfect' society and economy. A Progressive society is a top-down society where government makes decisions that significantly influence, or explicitly direct, the behaviours of individuals.

Enduring philosophies have anchors

Enduring political philosophies have anchors. A philosophical anchor helps inform how and why policy positions should be taken. The problem with Progressivism is that it lacks an anchor. Classical liberals approach politics and public policy anchored by maximising individual freedom through limited coercive government. Conservatism's anchors are existing traditions, culture and institutions. Labourism is anchored by advancing the best interests of working people within a relatively classical liberal framework. Even communism has an anchor of equality through the empowerment of the state and undermining individual liberty. These anchors can be subjective, but they have relative clarity.

The same cannot be said of Progressivism. At best, Progressivism's anchor is fairness through the use of government power. But fairness for whom? Taxes can be cut in fairness to working people. Taxes can be increased in fairness to poorly paid people. Fairness is a completely amorphous concept that can be twisted and abused to justify just about any action. According to Progressives, when one section of the economy or society becomes too powerful, the role of government is to decrease their power. Conversely, when one section becomes too vulnerable, the role of the government is to promote their interests.

There is no overlap between liberal democracy and Progressive political thought. Liberal democracy views the role of the individual as the primary agent for the affairs of society, the economy and government. Progressivism views the individual as a movable chess piece in fulfilling the ambitions of society, the economy and government. British economist Adam Smith exposed the fallacy of the style of thinking that supports Progressivism in his *Theory on Moral Sentiments*. According to Smith:

> The man of system, on the contrary, is apt to be very wise in his own conceit; and is often so enamoured with the supposed beauty of his own ideal plan of government ... He goes on to establish it completely and in all its parts, without any regard either to the great interests, or to the strong prejudices which may oppose it. He seems to imagine that he can arrange the different members of a great society with as much ease as the hand arranges the different pieces upon a chess-board. He does not consider that the pieces upon the chess-board have no other principle of motion besides that which the hand impresses upon them; but that, in the great chess-board of human society, every single piece has a principle of motion of its own, altogether different from that which the legislature might chuse to impress upon it.

Progressivism views the economy and society as a playing field where individual actors live out their lives. Under progressivism the role of government is not to act as an umpire. Progressivism views the government as the empowered manipulator of an economic and societal playing field with a dashboard of policy levers and dials that can be tweaked to constantly change its balance. The government's grand perspective is top-down, disconnected and operates with imperfect, verging on absent, information on the justifications of individual decisions.

This approach to government brings with it a sneering contempt from those in positions of centralised authority to any individual who chooses to buck their preferred trend, and their recourse is dehumanising rules and regulations that strip people of their individuality and their choices in the name of a greater good. This attitude is now omnipresent with politicians, bureaucrats and central planners who dictate what, how and where we can consume, play and engage in enterprise.

This is not a new phenomenon. As American historian, William E Leuchtenburg, argued in PBS's documentary *Prohibition*: 'It was a movement that was embraced by Progressives who thought of this as a fundamental kind of reform, in part because alcoholism was such a terrible problem and a particularly terrible problem for the working class, for the immigrant poor.'

The central tenet of Progressivism's advocacy for prohibition was that individuals, left to their own devices, particularly the poor and immigrants, could not make rational choices for themselves. Worse, the societal impact of their choices made their freedom expensive and justifiably disposable. This approach conflicts strongly with the bottom-up approach adopted by liberal democrats that respects individuals and their choices by allowing for society, the economy and government to be governed by the disaggregated decisions of millions of people. Classical liberals recognised that the coercive role of the state made it a dangerous institution because it allowed those in power to impose their will on the public.

The role of government in the foundations of a liberal democracy is to create the framework for individuals to go about their lives and enterprise. Unpacked to its most simple elements, government creates a framework by establishing predictable laws about the definition and protection of private property and contracts, courts to fairly adjudicate disputes and a policing mechanism to enforce them. Outside of these principles the role of the state is to do what the private sector cannot or will not, ranging from defending the nation's borders to managing foreign relations and taxation. The role of human rights is to protect the individual from the abuse of state power. Of course, in a modern context, for both good and bad reasons, a liberal democracy is more complex, but the evolution of modern democracy has come from these foundations.

As a result, individuals are held to account for themselves and their own future, no one individual or group can seize the arm of government to unnecessarily impose their will, enterprise generates wealth and the development of civil society creates an unseen foundation for societal welfare. But without a philosophical anchor, Progressivism simply becomes a political philosophy of using the power of government to do whatever is assumed to work at the time, often with inconsistent and incoherent results.

Progressives lash businesses that advocate a more competitive tax system so they can be internationally competitive and create sustainable jobs because it is 'unfair', and then bail out multinational car companies with subsidies that come from the pockets of working Australians to 'protect jobs'. Progressives have been quicker to rally for humane treatment of animals before people, as was amply demonstrated when a Progressive activist group ran a campaign to stop live cattle exports after ABC1 *4 Corners* ran a program showing animal mistreatment. Yet, they concurrently ignored the human cost of stopping affordable protein sources flowing into one of the world's developing countries.

Concerned Progressives advocate higher environmental standards through taxes and regulations that increase the cost of building new homes. Similarly, Progressives oppose development in their local communities under the banner that it undermines heritage and street character which protects established owners and reduces housing supply. But they are concurrent critics of high housing prices that disproportionately hit the young and poor who are unable to afford to buy into the market.

Progressives also advocate the introduction of 'environmentally justified' regulatory costs through renewable energy targets, carbon taxes and solar rebates. These increase the price of electricity. But, Progressives discount the fact that the only people sufficiently financially well off to avoid costs associated with these schemes are the wealthy. The wealthy can afford to replace equipment, and in the case of solar panels, make upfront payments for installations. In almost all cases the poor pay or are the least capable of paying.

Progressives oppose consumption based taxes, including the GST, because they disproportionately impact on families that spend a disproportionate amount of their disposable income on food, groceries and other consumables. Concurrently, Progressives argue for an unending number of new taxes on consumer items to tackle food, alcohol and tobacco consumption and gaming, as well as any other public policy objective they deem worthy. And the result of these taxes is exactly the same as consumption taxes that disproportionately hit the less well-off. Finally, Progressives are the first to assert that women should have the right to make decisions about their own bodies and strongly oppose any government regulation on abortion. But they are some of the most vehement advocates for more regulation around the harmful consumption behaviours of individuals.

Most political philosophies provide sufficient anchors so that adherents are able to articulate and justify their policies. For Progressives the justifications can range from 'fairness', to 'equity', to 'human rights', to 'social justice', to 'keep the cost to government down', to 'benefiting society', to 'respecting individual choice'.

No consistent thread

All political philosophies have consistency and shades of grey. The test is whether a position can be founded in a consistent philosophy. With Progressives there is no common thread, like 'preserving institutions', or 'maximising liberty', or 'empowering workers'.

Without a consistent thread every policy based on what is perceived to work carries the risk of unintended consequences. If the government caps salaries, it has the unintended consequence of discouraging talent. If the government enforces standards of service, it prices people out of access. If government regulates a type of behaviour, it may create a black market. And with every new problem, the solution is more taxes, laws or regulations. But you cannot out-regulate the problems of regulation.

In practice Progressivism is a political ideology to justify technocracy where data is used to constantly justify the expansion of government and the corrosion of individual freedom and human rights. Considering it is a political philosophy that represents itself as favouring the disenfranchised, in practice it centralises power within the hands of a small group of technocrats. Sadly this technocratic approach is now seeping into our society where models and data are used to inform 'evidence-based policy' without any proper consideration of whether it is the role of government to interfere in the first place.

What is most alarming is that Progressivism's shortcomings are neither novel, nor unpractised. Many of the failed grand experiments of the 20th century had their roots in Progressive ideals and seeded ruinous consequences for society, the economy and human liberty. Rather than being a forward-looking political philosophy, Progressivism is merely the latest incarnation of tried, tested and failed political ideals rooted in the idea that human nature is a scourge that should be overcome, rather than unleashed to advance the maximum potential of individuals, and consequently society and the economy.

Contributors

David Archibald is a Perth-based scientist working in the fields of oil exploration, climate science and medical research. He is a Visiting Fellow, Institute of World Politics in Washington, DC where he teaches a course in Strategic Energy Policy.

Barry Cohen AM, businessman, was the federal member for Robertson from 1969 until his retirement before the 1990 election. He was Minister for the Environment from 1983 until 1987 in the Hawke Government. He is the author of nine books of political anecdotes; the latest is *Bringing the House Down*.

Peter Day was a New York and Washington correspondent for *The Australian*, and has been widely published in international and Australian journals and newspapers. Since marrying in Cairo 26 years ago, he has travelled extensively in Egypt and has recently written about that country for *The Spectator* and *Quadrant*.

Kevin Donnelly is Director of the Melbourne-based Education Standards Institute. He taught for 18 years in government and non-government secondary schools and has been a member of various curriculum bodies. His Doctoral thesis defends a liberal-humanist view of education.

James Franklin is Professor of Mathematics and Statistics at the University of New South Wales. His books include *What Science Knows: And How It Knows It*; *The Science of Conjecture*; and *Corrupting the Youth: A History of Philosophy in Australia*. His recent work is on extreme risks and the philosophy of mathematics.

Ian Harper is Emeritus Professor of The University of Melbourne and a director of Deloitte Access Economics. He is a lay member of the Anglican Church of Australia and author of the 2011 Australian Christian Book of the Year, *Economics for Life*.

John Humphreys is an economist with experience at the Commonwealth Treasury, international consulting, and policy-based research. He has published on topics ranging from trade policy to climate economics to civil society. John is currently the director of the Human Capital Project while also completing his PhD in economics.

Michael James is an editor and writer based in the UK. From 1994 to 1998 he was the founding editor of *Agenda*, the policy journal of the College of Business and Economics at the Australian National University.

Gary Johns is a columnist for *The Australian* newspaper, and author of *Aboriginal Self-Determination: the Whiteman's Dream* and *Right Social Justice: Better Ways to Help the Poor*. He was a minister in the Keating Government, senior fellow at the Institute of Public Affairs, and an associate professor at the Australian Catholic University.

Eric Jones is Professor Emeritus of La Trobe University and sometime Professorial Fellow, Melbourne Business School, University of Melbourne, as well as formerly Honorary Archivist, Royal Australasian Ornithologists' Union. He is the author of books and articles on world, economic, agricultural and environmental history.

Asher Judah is the Deputy Executive Director of the Property Council of Australia (Victoria). He was a contributing author to the book, *Right Social Justice: Better Ways to Help the Poor*, and has been published in Australia's newspapers and opinion websites. He is also an active member of the Australia India Business Council.

Miranda Kiraly is a Bachelor of Laws student at Victoria Law School. She has previously worked in federal politics as a speechwriter and researcher. Since 2009, she has been a leading discussant for the Liberal Book Club.

Richard Lyons is the Associate Editor, IPA Review and a BA (Honours) student. His main area of research is ancient history and legal history.

David Martin Jones is an academic and writer based in Brisbane and London.

Greg Melleuish teaches history and politics at the University of Wollongong. His books include *Is the West Special? World History and Western Civilisation,* Institute of Public Affairs, 2012 and *The Power of Ideas,* Australian Scholarly Publishing 2009. During 2012 he edited *Policy* for the Centre for Independent Studies.

Frank Milne is BMO Chair in Economics and Finance in the Department of Economics, Queen's University, Canada. He has acted as a consultant for the Canadian Government, and was a Special Advisor at the Bank of Canada in 2008-09.

Kerryn Pholi is a former Aboriginal public servant and social worker. She has worked for various government agencies on data on Aboriginal health and wellbeing. Her articles on identity politics and freedom of speech have appeared in *Quadrant, Spectator Australia* and *The Drum.*

Tom Switzer is editor of the *Spectator Australia* and an adjunct fellow at the Institute of Public Affairs. He was opinion editor at *The Australian* (2001-08) and editorial writer at the *Australian Financial Review* (1998-01).

Cassandra Wilkinson is an author, commentator, columnist and co-founder and chair of FBi FM Sydney's Australian music radio station. Her book *Don't Panic – Nearly Everything is Better Than You Think* argued that the world is getting better. She is included in the anthology *Best Australian Science Writing 2012* (UNSW Press).

Tim Wilson is an international public policy analyst and commentator and is a policy director at the Institute of Public Affairs. He is a Senior Fellow at New York's Centre of Medicine in the Public Interest and a Director of Alfred Health. He previously worked in international aid and politics.